DANTE'S POETRY OF THE DONATI

BY
PIERO BOITANI

THE BARLOW LECTURES ON DANTE
DELIVERED AT UNIVERSITY COLLEGE LONDON
17–18 MARCH 2005

OCCASIONAL PAPERS, 7
Edited by John Lindon

MANEY PUBLISHING
FOR THE
SOCIETY FOR ITALIAN STUDIES

2007

PUBLISHED BY
THE SOCIETY FOR ITALIAN STUDIES
www.sis.ac.uk

© The Society for Italian Studies, 2007

All rights reserved. No part of this publication may be reproduced, stored in a retrieval system or transmitted in any form or by any means, electronic, mechanical, photocopying, recording or otherwise without the written permission of the copyright holder. Requests for such permission must be addressed to Permissions Section, Maney Publishing, who act on behalf of the Society.

Statements in *Dante's Poetry of the Donati* reflect the views of the author, and not those of the editor or the Society.

ISBN 978 0 9525901 7 0

Produced by Maney Publishing, Suite 1c, Joseph's Well, Hanover Walk, Leeds LS3 1AB, UK.
www.maney.co.uk

CONTENTS

FOREWORD

The year 2006, which has been marked by 250th anniversary celebrations for Mozart, also happens to be the 130th of the death in November 1876, at the composer's birthplace Salzburg, of Henry Clark Barlow, founder of the historic Barlow lectures on Dante, which were first held in 1877 after Barlow's will took effect bequeathing to University College London his Dante books and papers, and establishing annual courses of originally twelve Dante lectures.

Foremost among earlier lecturers were Edward Moore and Edmund Gardner. After the Second World War, during which they were suspended, they resumed on a biennial basis, which became triennial after the centenary, when they were chronicled in *Italian Studies*, XXXII. Between 1977 and 2002 they were given by Philip McNair (1979), Maria Corti (1987), Giorgio Padoan (1990), Robert Hollander (1993), Peter Dronke (1995, published in the present series of Occasional Papers), Zygmunt Barański (1998), and Bernhard König (2002), while in 1984 a round table was organized which brought together Lino Pertile, Peter Brand, Zygmunt Barański, Michael Caesar, and David Robey.

Last year we had the good fortune to hear Piero Boitani deliver the 'tryptich' published here, a fascinating exploration of Dante's presentation of the Donati, whose pervasive presence in the *Divina Commedia*, a comedy within the *Comedy*, mirrors their importance in the poet's life: Dante's wife, best friend, and (together with Pope Boniface VIII) arch enemy were all, of course, Donati. The subject would certainly have met with Barlow's approval: his own Dante papers typically focus on the historical dimension of the poem and include one arguing that 'colui / Che fece per viltà lo gran rifiuto' (*Inf.* III, 60) is not Esau, Pontius Pilate, or the abdicant hermit-pope Pietro da Morrone, but Messer Vieri dei Cerchi, the ineffectual leader (mentioned in these pages) of Dante's party, the White Guelfs, against the Black 'baron', Corso Donati.

We are grateful to Judith Bryce, Robert Gordon, and the Committee of the Society for Italian Studies for agreeing to publish this further set of Barlow Lectures in the Society's series of Occasional Papers.

John Lindon
University College London
November 2006

I
DISMAY: THE THIEVES*

The story of the Donati family during the Middle Ages is one of violence, fraud, theft, power games, and civic strife just as gripping as any of Shakespeare's historical plays or the popular fiction and television dramas of today. Several memorable characters, both male and female, stand out in the thirteenth-century chronicles of Florence, their lives and emotions interweaving with those of Dante Alighieri, and duly appearing in his *Commedia*, where they are democratically distributed among Hell, Purgatory, and Heaven.

A swift glance at the Donati family tree can help us understand their vital role in Florentine public life.[1] Traceable to 1065, when Fiorenzo 'the Baron' set up a hospital in the city, the Donati appear to have been wealthy enough even then to provide for the setting up of charitable institutions. They owned land, property, and mills beyond the city walls, a group of houses around a square known as 'corte dei Donati', and, in the fourteenth century, a tower and house in via San Martino. This house was joined to the one which belonged to Geri del Bello before passing to Alighiero, Dante's father, and it was here that Dante was born and grew up. The Donati family's importance is attested by the fact that their war trophies were on proud display in the Franciscan basilica of Santa Croce, and many of their bodies buried in the churches of Santa Margherita, Santa Croce, and Santa Reparata, this last later becoming Santa Maria del Fiore, the Cathedral of Florence.

The two branches of the family that interest us here descend from the eponymous Donato del Pazzo, who lived around 1158 and had two sons, Vinciguerra and Ubertino (the latter is mentioned in *Paradiso* XVI). Ubertino fathered Donato, whose son Manetto married Maria and produced several children, among them Gemma and Foresino. Gemma Donati became Dante's wife. Foresino's son, Niccolò, Dante's nephew by marriage, carefully guarded the interests of his aunt Gemma and Dante's children after the poet's exile, while Dante's father-in-law, Manetto, had helped Dante by acting as guarantor for several substantial loans he had taken out. The other branch of the family is even more interesting. Vinciguerra fathered Buoso (referred to in *Inferno* XXX) and his brother Forese, who married Gualdrada. This couple produced the Buoso mentioned in *Inferno* XXV and two further sons, Simone and Taddeo. Simone was the father of Dante's three contemporaries: Corso, Forese, and Piccarda. We know nothing, however, of the collocation within this family tree of the thief Cianfa Donati who appears in *Inferno* XXV.

Nothing better illustrates the part played by the Donati in the history of Florence than an episode found in the chronicles of the time (1215–1216) concerning Gualdrada, grandmother to Corso, Forese, and Piccarda. Buondelmonte dei Buondelmonti was betrothed to one of Lambertuccio degli Amidei's daughters.[2] One day, as he was passing by the Donati home, Gualdrada called to him from the balcony and, showing him one of her beautiful daughters, asked: 'Chi ài tu tolta per moglie? Io ti serbavo questa' ['Whom have you chosen as wife? I was keeping this one for you'].

Buondelmonte looked at the girl and was immediately attracted, but honourably replied: 'Non posso altro oramai' ['It is too late now to change']. Gualdrada assured him that this was far from the case, and promptly offered to pay the fine accruing for the broken promise. Buondelmonte thus abandoned his *promessa sposa* for Gualdrada and Forese's daughter. The Amidei were not amused, and took immediate revenge, beating him almost to pulp. The Uberti joined them, adding that they might as well do the job properly and kill him, since even a simple wound would leave a scar of hatred. 'Cosa fatta capo à', pronounced Mosca Lamberti on this occasion, as reported both in the chronicles and by Dante: 'what's done can't be undone'. Buondelmonte was murdered on Easter Sunday 1216, and Mosca's comment, as Dante records in *Inferno* XXVIII, became 'ill seed for the Tuscan people': by prompting Buondelmonte's murder, it became the source of the divisions and internal strife which were to be the curse of Florence for a century. The Buondelmonti, the Donati, and their friends formed a coalition against the Amidei and the Uberti, thirty-nine families, apparently, against thirty-three. 'O Buondelmonte', exclaims Dante's ancestor, Cacciaguida, in *Paradiso* XVI (ll. 140–41), 'quanto mal fuggisti | le nozze süe per li altrui conforti!' ['how ill for you that you fled its nuptials at another's bidding!']. It was thus Gualdrada Donati's prompting or advice that brought lasting and incalculable damage to Florence. After her fateful words from the balcony and the ensuing events, the two factions split definitively, taking from then on the names of Guelfs and Ghibellines.

The Donati were landed nobles. They lived off their rents and used their title to hold offices of prestige in other cities, as *podestà* or *capitani*. Like many members of their class, they practised no profession or scholarly pursuits, taking no interest whatsoever in any form of culture or literature (the poetic exchange between Forese and Dante apart). What they did was fight, often as *condottieri*, hired soldiers, or mercenaries. Nor were they averse to theft and fraud, fully deserving the nickname of 'malefami' by which they were known among the Florentine people. According to the anonymous compiler of the *Chiose Selmi*, Cianfa Donati, for example, was guilty of burglary and cattle-stealing. Buoso, who appears to have been the uncle of Corso, Forese, and Piccarda, was suspected of embezzlement.[3] Both appear among the thieves of *Inferno* XXV. In the *Tenzone con Forese Donati*, Forese is also accused by Dante of being a 'piùvico ladron': a 'public' or notorious thief.[4]

Simone Donati, the father of Forese, Corso, and Piccarda, was for his part responsible for an infamous act of fraud against this uncle Buoso, presumably brother of the Forese who married Gualdrada. He appears in *Inferno* XXX, where the commentators report the episode with after-dinner expansiveness, relishing it as a practical joke. The wealthy Buoso has died without a direct heir, and is laid out in bed. Fearing that he is intestate, his nephew Simone convinces Gianni Schicchi dei Cavalcanti (the 'goblin' of *Inferno* XXX) to take his dead uncle's place on the bed and, mimicking Buoso's appearance and manner, to dictate a will to a notary bequeathing Simone a good sum of money and his best mare, the one Dante calls (l. 43) 'la donna de la torma' ['the jewel of the stud'].

It was at the end of the thirteenth century, however, that the Donati, the source of the split between the Guelfs and the Ghibellines, again played a decisive role: this time, in dividing the Guelfs into Whites and Blacks. At the centre of the split, and of events in Florence for the next twenty years, was Corso Donati. Proudly Guelf, right from the start Corso opposed the Cerchi, a less ancient but wealthier family, who had bought the houses of the counts Guidi, which were near to his own. His animosity towards them was endless; their leader, Vieri — 'uomo bellissimo, ma di poca malizia, né di bel parlare' ['a most handsome man, but less than shrewd, and lacking in eloquence'] — he mocked as 'l'asino di Porta': 'Ha raghiato oggi l'asino di Porta' ['Has the ass of Porta brayed today?'], he would ask his men. But he did not stop at mockery. He also poisoned, or was suspected of poisoning, six young members of the rival family with pig's blood. After numerous brawls, the two factions finally fought it out at the May Day feast of 1300, when one of the Donati gang cut off Ricoverino de' Cerchi's nose. According to Dino Compagni, this blow 'fu la distruzione della nostra città' ['was our city's ruin'].[5] The whole of Florence then split into Whites (Cerchi) and Blacks (Donati). Absent from the May Day festivities, Corso flew into a rage. He had already dealt forcefully with his sisters, tearing Piccarda from the convent of Monticelli to give her in marriage to Rossellino della Tosa, and obliging Ravenna to leave the cloister so that he could obtain her inheritance for himself. He had been in favour of the alliance with Lucca and Genoa against the city of Pisa, later relenting, apparently after receiving money from Ugolino della Gherardesca (the betrayed traitor whose death by starvation is harrowingly told in *Inferno* XXXIII). He was frequently either *capitano* or *podestà*, in Bologna, Padua, Pistoia, and Parma; but was never absent at the crucial moments which mark Florence's internal and foreign affairs. He played a decisive role in the battle of Campaldino (in which Dante and Buonconte da Montefeltro also took part). He tried to have Guido Cavalcanti (whom Corso nicknamed 'Cavicchia' or 'Bolt') assassinated during a pilgrimage to St James of Compostela (Cavalcanti responded by shooting an arrow at Corso but was chased by his men and his hand wounded by the stones they threw at him).[6] He was vehemently opposed to government by the people and the Ordinances of Justice which restricted the magnates' power: he lorded it over the city for two full years, 1298 and 1299. In other words, Corso was an antecedent of the Machiavellian Prince: lion and fox, lord of scorn and derision, master of theft and speech. Here is how Dino Compagni depicted him in his famous account:

Uno cavaliere della somiglianza di Catellina romano, più crudele di lui, gentile di sangue, bello del corpo, piacevole parlatore, addorno di belli costumi, sottile d'ingegno, con l'animo sempre intento a malfare, col quale masnadieri si raunavano e gran séguito avea, molte arsioni e molte ruberie fece fare, e gran dannaggio a' Cerchi e a' loro amici; molto avere guadagnò, e in grande alteza salì. Costui fu messer Corso Donato che per sua superbia fu chiamato il Barone; che quando passava per la terra molti gridavano: 'Viva il Barone'; e parea la terra sua. La vanagloria il guidava, e molti servigi facea.[7]

[A nobleman similar to the Roman Catiline, more cruel than he, of noble blood, handsome in appearance, eloquent, adorned with fine attire, of subtle wit, his mind always plotting evil deeds; many robbers met with him and his following was large; frequently did he commission acts of arson and theft, with considerable damage to the Cerchi and their circle; he accumulated much wealth, and rose considerably in stature. Such was Messer Corso Donato who on account of his pride was called the Baron; when he rode through a place many there were who cried out 'Long live the Baron', and the whole city seemed to belong to him. His many deeds were guided by vainglory.]

On 2 May 1299 an uprising put a temporary halt to Corso's arrogance: he was fined and, refusing to pay, was banished. The Baron was undaunted. He approached the

Pope, Boniface VIII, and plotted against the people's government in Florence. He was condemned once more in his absence: this time to death, with his houses to be destroyed. In an attempt at impartiality and a peace settlement, the Florentine Priors who were elected in June 1300 (including Dante) banished seven leaders of the Whites (including Guido Cavalcanti) and eight Blacks. By this time, however, Florence's destiny was marked out. Events followed with terrifying speed as reported by Ciacco in the *Inferno*.[8] Boniface appointed first Matteo d'Acquasparta, then Charles of Valois as his peacemakers. The Whites attempted to remedy the situation by sending a papal embassy which included Dante. But on 3 November 1301, Charles arrived in Florence: Corso followed immediately, entering the city with a small band of men. He took the town, let his men sack it, and then ruled for more than three years. On 27 January 1302 the *Signoria* of the Blacks put Dante on trial in his absence and sentenced him to exile. Corso now wavered between the Blacks and the people's group, making him suspect to both parties. When he took as his third wife the daughter of the most feared Ghibelline captain, Uguccione della Faggiola, his enemies joined forces and on 6 October 1308, as the bells tolled, they declared him a traitor and ransacked his properties. He was forced to flee the city, but the commune's Catalan soldiers caught up with him and killed him just outside the city walls, near the convent of San Salvi.[9]

It comes as no surprise therefore that Dante, who had himself suffered on account of Corso's actions and saw him as the chief culprit of the 'woeful ruin' towards which Florence appeared to be heading,[10] imagines him falling to Hell directly at the very moment of death. The chroniclers relate that during his final flight, Corso fell from his horse and was killed, or that he fell deliberately and was struck by the mercenaries as he lay on the ground.[11] In his commentary on *Purgatorio* XXIV, Benvenuto adds that his foot got caught up in the stirrup, and the horse dragged him for some distance before the mercenaries slit his throat.[12] The prophecy in *Purgatorio* XXIV with which Forese predicts the death of his brother Corso, without as much as naming him, presents a striking sequence: tied to the horse's tail, Corso is first dragged, as was the punishment then given to traitors, 'inver' la valle ove mai non si scolpa' ['towards the valley where there is no absolving'], while the horse immediately afterwards turns into a 'beast of the apocalypse', a demon which increases in speed and size at every step, its size apparently increasing with its speed,[13] until it throws and stuns him with a kick, dashing him to the ground, 'vilmente disfatto' ['vilely undone']. First, an ineluctable fall to Hell, as though of the whole person; then an ignominious destruction of the body alone on earth. To paraphrase Blake, Death 'from a pale horse': an enormous whirling shadow in sharp contrast with the horse which closes the passage immediately afterwards. There, his brother Forese parts definitively from Dante, Virgil, and Statius with long strides and the appearance of a rider who boldly spurs his horse to a gallop, breaking away from a troop of armed men to launch the first assault on the enemy: 'qual esce alcuna volta di gualoppo | lo cavalier di schiera che cavalchi, | e va per farsi onor del primo intoppo'.[14]

*   *   *

The vision of Corso's imminent and ruinous fall takes us to Hell, and, from the reference to the horse-dragged traitor, we can even infer to which circle: as company for Ugolino, of course, who was said to have used his money to make Corso relent. Once in Purgatory, the vision impacts us violently backwards, projecting the shadow of the Baron throughout the 'valley where there is no absolving'. Shortly beforehand, Forese's words on Piccarda had opened up before us the Paradise which had welcomed her, Corso's victim. It could be said, therefore, that the three Donati siblings share a shrewdly distributed afterlife, with their spokesman Forese in the middle undergoing purification, thus predicting the two destinies of damnation and beatitude, and the unnamed Corso, speaking from the earth, condemning himself and sanctifying his sister. But it is in Hell, the place of unredeemed history, that the Donati are most prominent. Bereft of surname — perhaps the most fitting punishment for such a proud family — two of them frame canto XXV, summing up the whole dimension of theft and providing Dante with the cue for a piece of unrivalled skill in the *Commedia*: Cianfa and Buoso, whose names emerge almost by chance and who moreover have completely lost their identity, reduced as they are to mere bodies which turn into slimy, faceless animals.

I shall now try to follow the episode which Dante sets out before our astonished eyes in *Inferno* XXV. Vanni Fucci, the Pistoia thief, protagonist of canto XXIV, is still on the scene at the start of this next canto, and in fact opens it with a gesture seen nowhere else in the *Commedia*: after angrily predicting to Dante the imminent defeat of the Whites by the Blacks, he raises both hands with the obscene gesture of the 'figs', cursing God himself. A proud spirit — 'in Dio tanto superbo', more so than anyone else, even than Capaneus in *Inferno* XIV — Vanni is immediately punished: a serpent coils itself around his neck as if to suffocate him so that after his blasphemy he is unable to utter another word; another snake immobilizes his arms completely. The sinner then flees in silence. Immediately after this, another raging being appears, this time a centaur with its croup covered in more serpents than can be found in the whole Maremma. On its shoulders is a dragon with outspread wings and flames sprouting from its jaws, which burn anyone who ventures near it. The centaur approaches, calling out to Vanni, 'Ov'è, ov'è l'acerbo?' ['Where is he, where is the hardened wretch?']. As Virgil soon explains, the beast is in fact Cacus, who 'di sotto 'l sasso del monte Aventino, | di sangue fece spesse volte laco': 'many a time made a lake of blood beneath the rock of Mount Aventine', stealing Geryon's herd by fraud, for which he was later beaten to death by Hercules.

Shouting, silence, shouting; a man covered and bound by serpents, a monster crawling in snakes, and a dragon; a punishment inflicted by God, who silences Vanni, and a punishment inflicted by Hercules, the prefiguration of Christ, who puts an end to the 'opere biece' ['crooked ways'] of Cacus with his club: Virgil and Ovid, presiding together over the monster's story. The sequence is rapid and furious, and leads on to an even more astounding spectacle. After Vanni, Cacus too flees and, while Virgil is still speaking, three spirits appear, unnoticed by the two poets until they hear them shout out (adding to the general clamour), 'Who are you?' Neither Dante nor Virgil recognizes them, but one of them — as sometimes happens by chance, Dante writes — names a fourth person, saying 'Cianfa dove fia rimaso?' ['Where can Cianfa be?']. It is the first appearance of the *leitmotif* of recognition, which will become central in *Purgatorio* XXIII and *Paradiso* III. Placing a finger 'from chin to nose', Dante signals to Virgil to remain silent.

Another scene then opens, so extraordinary that the poet feels the need to warn the reader:

> Se tu se' or, lettor, a creder lento
> ciò ch'io dirò, non sarà meraviglia,
> ché io che 'l vidi, a pena il mi consento.
>
> [If, reader, you are now slow to credit
> what I shall tell, it will be no wonder,
> for I who saw it scarcely admit it to myself.]

This apostrophe marks the start of two metamorphoses. In the first a serpent with six claws, which is in fact Cianfa himself, rolls around one of the spirits and the two bodies merge into one monstrous entity, a hybrid never seen before, with 'una faccia, ov'eran due perduti' ['a single face, in which two were lost']. In the second metamorphosis, a man and a serpent exchange characteristics, each taking on the other's likeness while they observe each other, yawning, as though hypnotized, and smoke billows all around.

The details of this double metamorphosis are worthy of a horror film. In the first case the serpent attacks one of the three spirits, clamping itself around his belly with its middle claws and around his arms with its front claws, while gnawing his cheeks with its upper and lower fangs; it then spreads out its hind claws towards his thighs, thrusting its tail between them and curling it back over the loins of the condemned man. Recalling Ovid, Dante writes: 'ellera abbarbicata mai non fue | ad alber sì, come l'orribil fiera | per l'altrui membra avviticchiò le sue' ['Never was ivy so rooted to a tree as the horrid beast intertwined the other's members with its own']. These two bodies become stuck to each other as though they were 'hot wax', mixing their colours as when paper burns: before the flame across the paper spreads 'un color bruno | che non è nero ancora e 'l bianco more' ['a dark colour that is not yet black, and the white dies off']. Neither entity is now recognizable. The other two contemplate this monstrous being in astonishment, each shouting (two more shouts, simultaneously) 'Omè, Agnel, come ti muti! | Vedi che già non se' né due né uno' ['Alas! Agnello, how you change! Look, you are now neither two nor one!']. The second sinner is thus 'identified' — though the term hardly seems apt in the context — as Agnello dei Brunelleschi. But the name here counts for as much as Cianfa Donati's, mentioned shortly beforehand — for precisely nothing. The two heads become one and two 'figures' appear, in the same face, that of the serpent and that of the man: 'in una faccia, ov'eran due perduti', that is, in a single face, in which two were lost in their individuality and forever damned. From the monster's four limbs, the two arms of the man and the two front claws of the serpent, two arms are formed; thighs, legs, belly and chest become 'membra che non fuor mai viste' ['such members as were never seen']. All former appearance is thus cancelled and in the end 'the perverted shape', which seems simultaneously two and nothing, moves away — after all the previous speed — 'with slow pace'.

But this slowness is merely a brief pause, in a canto of incredible speed. It is soon followed by a flash, like a lizard darting from side to side of the street in the blazing heat of summer. Just as the lizard appears like 'lightning' when it darts from one hedge to the next, so 'a small, fiery serpent',[15] 'livid, and black as a pepper-corn',[16] heads straight for the bellies of the other two spirits, transfixing the navel of one of them, then falling stretched out on the ground. The 'transfixed' man stares at the snake without a word, but, standing still, yawns, as though sleep or fever had come over him. He continues to look at the snake (and the snake at him) while smoke billows from the wound of the one and the mouth of the other, and the two clouds of smoke merge. At this Dante pauses to utter his *vanto* ['vaunt'] over Lucan and Ovid, the two masters of poetic metamorphosis:

> Taccia Lucano omai là dov'e' tocca
> del misero Sabello e di Nasidio,
> e attenda a udir quel ch'or si scocca.
>   Taccia di Cadmo e d'Aretusa Ovidio,
> ché se quello in serpente e quella in fonte
> converte poetando, io non lo 'nvidio;
> ché due nature mai a fronte a fronte
> non trasmutò sì ch'amendue le forme
> a cambiar lor matera fosser pronte.

> [Let Lucan now be silent with his tales
> of wretched Sabellus and Nasidius,
> and let him wait to hear what now comes forth!
> Let Ovid be silent about Cadmus and Arethusa;
> for if in his poetry he turns him into a serpent and
> her into a fountain, I do not grudge him it,
> for two natures face to face
> he never so transmuted that both kinds
> were ready to exchange their substance.]

Following these 'rules of transmutation', the serpent's tail forks into two while the man's feet, legs and thighs mould together. The forked tail of the serpent becomes two legs, its skin softens, while the man's skin hardens. The human arms retract at the armpits and the serpent's claws lengthen as the man's legs shorten. The beast's hind-legs entwine and become a penis, while two feet emerge from the man's penis. The smoke clouding both creatures gives them a new colour, making hair grow on one of them and stripping the other of hair. The serpent-man rises; the man-serpent falls: neither taking its eyes — the 'lucerne empie', the 'baleful lamps' — off the other, while the 'snout' of each changes. The serpent-man, standing upright, draws in his face towards the temples, and from the 'troppa matera', the over-abundant matter accumulated at that point, ears emerge from the bare cheeks; what is left goes to make the nose and thicken the lips. The man-serpent, now lying down, pushes out his snout, pulls his ears into his head as a snail does with its horns; and, previously whole and fit for speech, his tongue divides, while that of the serpent-man, previously forked, joins up into a single tongue. The transformation now complete, the smoke stops. The soul turned into a serpent flees through the valley with a hiss which fills two lines of the Italian text with *f* and *s* sounds: 'L'anima ch'era *f*iera divenuta, | *s*uffolando *s*i *f*ugge per la valle' ['the soul that was become a brute fled hissing along the valley']. Speaking now, the serpent-become-man spits after it (the '*s*puta' — and its English counterpart *spit* — with the plosive sonority of the *p* and *t*, in complete opposition to the initial sibilants), and, turning his back to him, says to the third soul: 'I' vo' che Buoso corra, | com' ho fatt'io, carpon per questo calle' ['I'll have Buoso run on all fours, as I have done, along this road'].

With the mention of the name Buoso, the other Donati of this canto, the 'mutare e trasmutare', the 'change and interchange', of the seventh *bolgia* or 'ballast' ('settima zavorra') are over, and the poet invokes the 'newness' of the scene to excuse the fact that his pen has lacked precision. Although his eyes are now confused and his soul lost — bewildered ('smagato') — the character Dante still manages to recognize the two spirits in flight: Puccio dei Galigai, known as the Cripple, the only one of the three to escape metamorphosis; the other, Francesco Cavalcanti, murdered by the men of Gaville, the village that was later subjected to retaliation by Cavalcanti's kinsmen and came to regret the murder: 'l'altr'era quel che tu, Gaville, piagni' ['the other was the man for whom you, Gaville, do mourn']. With a line all the more lapidary for its obliqueness, the canto ends: only to be accomplished — in a kind of enjambment between sections which picks up the opening invective against Pistoia — at the beginning of the next canto, in the invective against Florence: famous on sea, on land, and in Hell because of the five thieves who up to this point have occupied the stage.

*   *   *

Florence clearly dominates the episode. Proof of this is the violent prophecy which ends canto XXIV, when Vanni Fucci predicts the banishment of the Whites. Moreover, the imagery out of which canto XXV takes shape — smoke and serpents — recurs in Dante's letter to Henry VII, in which Florence, which 'exhales pestilential fumes, evaporating its corrupt mood', is compared to a viper that attacks the belly of its mother, Rome, even though made in her likeness.[17]

None the less, Florence (and the Donati) are only a starting point for Dante's strategy in *Inferno* XXIV–XXV. The first and more important of his aims is obviously to hold up to perpetual mockery the sin of theft, and not simply theft (which Puccio the Cripple, the only sinner not to undergo metamorphosis, is guilty of), but theft with fraud, 'grievous theft', which Thomas Aquinas classified according to three types: sacrilege (Vanni Fucci), embezzlement (Cianfa and Agnello), and plagiary (Buoso and Francesco Cavalcanti). Such fraud is of course a social ill, violating the individual's right to possess and utilize things; in short — as indeed the situation in Florence shows — it can disrupt order and peace within the community.[18] But it is also, as an expression of greed, an ethical blow against justice and wilful neglect of the providential plan incarnated by Fortune, which governs the permutations of 'vain goods' and whose judgement is 'occulto come in terra l'angue' ['hidden like the snake in the grass'].[19] Finally, it is a sin against God, because the 'natural dominion over other creatures, which appertains to man according to reason, of which the image of God consists, is made manifest in the very creation of man', following the account of Genesis: 'Let us make man in our image, after our likeness: and let them have dominion over the fish of the sea, and over the fowl of the air …'.[20] 'Thus, those who push the natural desire for possession beyond what is right, or remove by theft that which should by rights belong to others, betray in themselves the image of God, straying from the divine likeness and transforming their very nature as human beings'.[21]

Here, therefore, lies the germ of the *contrappasso* governing the transmutations which the thieves undergo in *Inferno* XXIV–XXV. It is, of course, far from accidental that the three metamorphoses described by Dante in these passages are immediately directed towards serpents: because the passage in Genesis itself cited by St Thomas continues: 'dominion over the fish of the sea, and over the fowl of the air, and over the cattle, and over all the earth, and *over every creeping thing that creepeth upon the earth*'. Unique, therefore, and terribly appropriate is the revenge which the power of God invoked to punish Vanni Fucci levies ('croscia') on the thieves, making serpents the lords of men, whereas men should have dominated the reptiles. And even more severe when one thinks that the serpent was made to crawl over the earth while mankind had been provided with — as Peter Lombard points out with the words of Bede — 'erect stature'.[22]

As a creature 'more subtle than any beast of the field which the Lord God had made', the serpent has long been an icon of evil (and the devil, from Revelation to Augustine), particularly of trickery and fraud. This has been the case ever since the scene of temptation in the Earthly Paradise, after which God curses the serpent and forces it to crawl on its belly and to eat dust:[23] naked and terrified, like Adam and Eve after original sin, are the people who run among this 'cruel and most dismal swarm' of reptiles — 'the fearful throng of serpents' — which entirely fills the seventh ditch of Hell.[24] And Vanni Fucci, the spirit most 'in Dio … superbo' ['arrogant against God'] seen by Dante in all Hell, more so even than Capaneus (*Inferno* XII), merely follows in the footsteps of 'the first proud spirit', Lucifer: for both of them the *Commedia* uses the adjective 'acerbo', literally, 'unripe'.[25] Thus, what dominates Dante's theological-poetic imagination when he invents the punishment for the thieves is, beyond all other biblical and literary influences which may have contributed,[26] the dual primordial scene: Creation and the Fall.

Dante's mind, however, is never univocal: inspired by the Scriptures, he is equally inspired by the classics, and just as Vanni Fucci's posture resembles that of Virgil's Laocoon,[27] Cacus, the monster which oversees the circle of the thieves, is equally Virgilian. In *Aeneid* VIII, from this half-man's mouth black fires and thick smoke belch forth; he is chased by Hercules, 'fear lending wings to his feet'; and when the hero unblocks the entry to his den, it is 'as if the earth through some convulsion had gaped apart, unlocking the deepest dwellings of the infernal world': by casting Cacus straight into Hell, Dante perverts his nature, transforming him (and thus transmuting the Virgilian original) into a centaur, a winged dragon towering over it and vomiting flames, its croup crawling with snakes.[28] He then has Virgil himself relate his death according to Ovid's account in the *Fasti*.[29] But Dante will most certainly not have failed to notice that Evander, who recounts the end of Cacus in Virgil's poem, announces the providential intervention of Hercules with the sentence, 'attulit et nobis aliquando optantibus aetas | auxilium adventumque dei' ['time at last brought to us, as it has to others, an answer to our prayers for aid in the arrival of a god']; and that Servius, commenting on the two lines which follow — 'For Hercules himself, the supreme avenger, came; and came at his time of exultation, when he had lately slain and despoiled three-bodied Geryon' — glosses *ultor* ['avenger'] with 'non tantum noster, sed omnium terrarum' ['not only for us but for the whole world']. It would not have been difficult therefore to interpret Virgil's Hercules, predecessor and *typos* of Aeneas, and 'saviour' according to a view already widely held in classical culture, as the 'shadow' of Christ, whose advent and assistance against the Serpent's doings fulfil those of the 'avenger' for all mankind against the monsters of fraud Cacus and Geryon (who in fact, like Cacus, appears in Malebolge).[30] A man awaiting Emperor Henry VII as the Lamb of God, criticizing him for behaving like Hercules with the heads of the Hydra, would certainly have understood.[31] In other words, alongside the themes of Creation and the Fall (and the birth of Rome), the theme of Incarnation also begins to emerge indirectly in Dante, culminating in parodic inversion later in the canto when the 'perverted shape', blotting out every former feature — accomplishing the distorted form of the diviners which had brought the tears to Dante's eyes in *Inferno* XX — seems to foreshadow by contrast 'nostra effige' ['our likeness'], as depicted in the circle of the second person of the Trinity, the reflected light of *Paradiso* XXXIII.

When we reach the central episode of the canto, however, the double metamorphosis of the thieves, Dante's inspiration derives from Ovid and Lucan. At first the reference is implicit: on the one hand there is a hidden quotation from Ovid's account of Hermaphroditus and Salmacis in the simile of the ivy rooted to the tree and in the images of the two heads become one and the two shapes blended into one face; then, on the other, through the *Pharsalia*'s influence on the comparison with wax.[32] The second instance is explicit, with the famous *vanto*, or *Überbietung* (outbidding), over even Lucan and Ovid, the historical and mythic aspects of metamorphosis: the first for Sabellus's turning into ash and Nasidius's swelling until every human semblance is lost after a poisonous snake-bite; on the second, for transforming Cadmus and Arethusa into serpents.[33]

With anatomical precision and glacial imperturbability, Dante here shows how far the 'uncanny' can reach: as far as that supreme and demoniacal perversion of beauty and art which reveals our baser instincts. Some have referred to this as an 'aesthetics of the obscene', and of course the implicit reference to Hermaphroditus and the explicitly sexual images of the snake's tail stretching behind the sinner's loins, and the penises taking shape all belong to the sphere of eroticism and what Dante would have considered its perverse aspect.[34] But we must be wary about taking the poet's detachment as mere sadistic cruelty. Like the decorators of medieval cathedrals and manuscripts, Dante would never have contemplated the display of ugliness or perversion as an end in itself. On the contrary, he would have thought that the ugly, the base, serves to remind us of the supreme Beauty which we tend to forget and, since we cannot rest in or yield to ugliness, to urge us towards the beautiful and true.[35] He would have believed that, although sin disrupts the order of the world, punishment by God restores its defaced beauty and that even the damned are placed in Hell according to a law of harmony.[36] In short, he would have believed that all the horrendous matters he describes in *Inferno* XXIV–XXV would be meaningful only within the overall economy of the *Commedia* and that they would thus have to be interpreted in the light of what he was later to reveal in *Purgatorio* and *Paradiso*.

And indeed there is no doubt that the sexually-tinged transformations of *Inferno* XXV anticipate by contrast the theme of human procreation in the parallel canto of *Purgatorio* XXV,[37] where Statius offers a lengthy and remarkable explanation as to how part of a man's blood acquires within the heart the 'virtute informativa' ['ability to give shape'] to all its bodily members, thereafter descending purified, as sperm, towards the part 'ov'è più bello tacer che dire' ['where silence is fitter than speech'], the male sexual organs, then trickles into a woman's 'natural vessel' and there joins with female blood to form a clot which becomes a foetus. The whole process seems distorted in the thieves' hermaphroditic and parahomosexual metamorphoses: they have no ability to give any shape but are forced to assume one which is alien. The opposition between the two scenes reaches its climax at two different points: when the fiery serpent, livid and black as a peppercorn, penetrates one of the sinners at the navel, the part 'onde prima è preso nostro alimento' ['from which our food is first taken'][38] and when the hind claws of the serpent become 'lo membro che l'uom cela' ['the member man conceals'] while two snake claws sprout from the man's penis. The aesthetic norm of decency — 'ov'è più bello tacer che dire' — is quite irrelevant here. Procreation on the one hand, therefore, and sterile combining on the other: the forming of a human being — from a 'foetus', with God supplying the soul, to 'child' — in *Purgatorio*; spiralling fusion, feral entwining, loss and total annihilation, the 'generation' of one which is two and no one, in *Inferno*.

But not even this is enough for Dante. For it is obvious that alongside the theme of generation[39] lies the other theme evoked by contrast in *Inferno* XXIV–XXV, that of the resurrection of the body.[40] The burning, fall, and resurgence of Vanni Fucci are a clear distortion of this, all the more so as they are accompanied by the simile of the death and rebirth of the Phoenix which, while also described by Ovid in the *Metamorphoses*, are traditionally seen as symbols standing for the risen Christ.[41] The rising and falling of the damned in the second transformation of *Inferno* XXV take up the theme once more, while the similes move from the sublimity of the phoenix to the speed of the lizard under the summer heat and to the snail drawing its horns inside its shell, and the new creatures formed by the resurrection are not single, finally complete, individuals — as Christian doctrine preaches of those who will rise on the last day — but human-snake and snake-human hybrids. The very obsession with numbers in *Inferno* XXV[42] (an incessant sequence which starts from three–one and returns to its inverse, one–three, after passing through no fewer than thirteen divisions, fusions, and subdivisions of one, two, and zero)[43] seems to constitute a terrifying parody of 'quell'uno e due e tre che sempre vive / e regna sempre in tre e 'n due e 'n uno' ['That One and Two and Three who ever lives and ever reigns in Three and in Two and in One'] sung three times by each of the spirits in the Heaven of the Sun in preface to Solomon's discourse on the resurrection of the blessed in *Paradiso* XIV. And the dark colour preceding the flame and edging across the burning paper, not yet black and no longer white, makes for a pregnant infernal counterpoint to the brightness ('chiarezza') of resurrection celebrated by Solomon himself: to the ardour (of charity, repeated three times), to the light, finally to the white glow, the 'vivo candor', by which the coal that produces a flame outshines it, thus becoming the image of the resurrected flesh which will surpass the existing radiance of the spirit.[44]

We should not be surprised, therefore, if the bestial metamorphoses of *Inferno* XXV, which lead unerringly to the confusion of natures, find their sublime antithesis in Dante's 'trasumanar', passing beyond humanity, when he first goes up into Paradise (for which once again he uses an episode from Ovid's *Metamorphoses*, this time the myth of Glaucus) and, at the height of his journey through the afterlife, in the simultaneous transformation of the pilgrim and of the one image becoming three (the supreme Triune, or Three-in-One): 'una sola parvenza, | mutandom'io, a me si travagliava' ['the one sole appearance, I myself changing, was, for me, transformed'].[45] *Inferno* XXIV–XXV thus obliquely contain the experience of human life and the world in its entirety: from generation to death (the return to dust of Vanni Fucci), from

Creation to the Fall, from Incarnation to the Resurrection, from the metamorphosis of man into serpent, the icon of Evil, to the metamorphosis of man into something beyond the human, capable of contemplating the mystery of the Trinity.

The seventh bolgia is entirely taken up by such uncanny episodes of 'mutare e trasmutare', accompanied by shouts and silences, by swift movements and transfixed stillness, by yawns and smoke, by sleep and fever, in short by a continuous changing which seems to imitate the turns and the unstoppable flow of Time.[46] Yet on the other hand a set of highly precise 'norme' or laws are displayed in perverse arithmetical precision: a paradox within the paradox, because no logic can, strictly speaking, truly govern metamorphosis, particularly if we consider the philosophical, or rather, meta-physical absurdity proclaimed by canto XXV when Dante announces his wish to change two natures simultaneously 'sì ch'amendue le *forme* | a cambiar lor *matera* fosser pronte', so that both kinds may be ready to exchange their substance. Indeed, according to Aristotelian-Scholastic philosophy, form is 'that which imprints on the raw matter its specific essence, lending it individuality',[47] and it is difficult to see how this essence might change substance without complete loss — as in fact happens to the thieves — of its own nature.[48] And to return for a moment to the spheres of Creation and Fall to which the punishment of these sinners alludes, it is common medieval doctrine, summed up by Peter Lombard, that the self-image according to which God created man 'pertains to *form*', the 'likeness' 'to *nature*'.[49]

The deliberate overturning of the metaphysical and divine laws in which Dante believes is emphasized by the image of the serpent and the condemned man stuck to each other like — and the simile appears perfectly natural — 'hot wax'. The tempera-ture of the wax is the crux here, as it is for Icarus in *Inferno* XVII.[50] For Dante claims that under the right conditions, 'come cera da suggello, ... la figura impressa non trasmuta': 'as the wax by the seal, ... the imprinted figure does not change'.[51] The thieves in his hell, one must therefore deduce, possess no 'seal', no divine imprinting, and no human form: they are also — another sexual perversion — far too ready, as 'matter', to desire alien form 'come la femmina ha desiderio del maschio', as a woman desires a man.[52]

All the similes in the canto are in fact inspired by the same feeling for nature:[53] the ivy rooted to the tree, the hot wax, the dark colour edging its way across the burning paper, the lizard, the peppercorn, the snail withdrawing its horns. The mimesis is perfect throughout; a sound realism rules the poet's mind. Yet as soon as we start to consider the similes in context, it becomes clear that they are divided into two distinct categories. In the first, fourth, and fifth the correspondence between the tenor and the vehicle is ensured by the fact that they both belong to the animal or vegetable kingdom. It may come as some surprise — though this is in any case part of the poet-reader game of expectancy — to see a serpent coiling itself around a man like ivy, darting about like a lizard, and with the colour of a peppercorn, but both comparisons are acceptable. In fact they add to our perception of the phenomenon. In the other similes Dante's marvellous naturalism is restricted to the second term of comparison, namely, the wax becoming sticky when hot, the dark stain edging its way across the burning paper, and the snail withdrawing its horns into its shell. None of these phenomena, however, properly belongs to human beings.

Dante deliberately introduces an increasing degree of alienation into his narrative: wax, papyrus, snail. The sequence culminates, of course, in the last of these. But at that point (l. 132) the natural shapes of human and serpent are so entwined that the boldness of the simile is reduced. It is in the images of the wax and paper that the effect of displacement reaches its climax. And while there are, as we have seen, serious philosophical reasons for the former, it is the liminality of the latter which strikes us more. Dante chooses not the moment in which the paper burns, but the moment immediately before. It is at this point that 'a dark colour that is not yet black' edges its way across the paper, 'and the white dies off'. Before the flame, the burning changes the appearance (in Scholastic terms, the 'accidens') of matter: no longer white, not yet black, but dark. This mixed colour and spreading dark halo are the culmination of what in *Inferno* XXV can only be referred to as *unheimlich* — uncanny.[54] This is what Cianfa Donati and Agnello Brunelleschi are reduced to: a piece of paper blackened by the approaching flame.

Moreover, the climax of alienation is reached in the second metamorphosis not so much by the stark horror of the limbs merging together, separating and multiplying, but more in the 'new colour' with which the smoke veils the man-serpent and the serpent-man. This, rather fittingly, comes between the two phases of transformation: because the suspended uncertainty which prevails once again calls into question the outcome, terrifying but already acquired by the first phase, and suggests even more horrifying consequences for the second. Indeed, the very metamorphosis opens with that supreme moment of giddy confusion represented by the staring eyes, the temporary immobility, the yawn, and, of course, the smoke: yawning which comes on with drowsiness or fever but *is* neither one nor the other and may be the effect of either, smoke which follows burning and darkens everything.[55]

The simile of the blackening paper is part of a series of passages in cantos XXIV–XXV devoted to writing and poetry.[56] The series begins with Vanni Fucci who is set alight and burns, in XXIV, so rapidly that 'né O sì tosto mai né I si scrisse' ['never was *I* or *O* written so fast'], and is touched on once again in canto XXV when Dante invites his reader to suspend disbelief before the spectacle of the seventh ditch ('se tu se' or, lettore, a creder lento'). Although he has seen what he is writing about, he barely allows himself to believe what he has seen. The strangeness of the formulation (curious when one thinks that its purpose is to lend truth to a narrative fiction) re-emerges soon after, in Dante's *vanto* over Lucan and Ovid. Again, it is the poet speaking: inviting Lucan to wait to hear 'what now comes forth' ('quel ch'or si scocca'), what his mind, as though it were a bow, now shoots like an arrow; and proclaiming that he bears no grudge towards Ovid if in his poem he turns Cadmus into a serpent and Arethusa into a fountain. Dante is perfectly aware that these are *poetic* metamorphoses, and it is on this level that he places his own. The two classical writers belong, like Virgil, to the 'bella scola' of Limbo, and it is already significant that during the canto Dante should silence all three while 'transforming' them, 'transmuting them in writing poetry' — 'converte poetando'.[57]

Inferno XXV thus contains a poetics of metamorphosis:[58] on the one hand it consists of re-writing, and on the other of treating *filth* in such a way that, as through a transformation, it gives rise to an ethical meditation upon recent history (Donati, Brunelleschi, Galigai, Cavalcanti) and a projection, as it were, against the light of the plot which runs throughout universal History (Creation, Fall, Incarnation, Resurrection), the events of mankind (generation, death, and rebirth), and man's deepest essence (nature, form, and matter), and the metamorphoses of Dante himself on the path towards God ('trasumanar' and the final 'travagliarsi'). It is because of this that the changing and interchanging of the seventh ditch are so important and incessant. This is also why Dante makes the final poetic *excusatio*: 'e qui mi scusi | la novità se fior la penna abborra' ['and let the newness of it be my plea if in anything my pen be at fault']. The *novità* is the entire series of metamorphoses presented throughout the canto. And before them even the most precise pen, like the maniacally precise one Dante uses here, is a little unsteady: an imperfect producer, he assembles things as best he can.

But 'abborra', the term Dante uses in his plea, does not express solely the 'imperfezione della cosa', the thing's imperfection. Some ancient commentators trace it to *aberrare*, to wander, to become lost and bewildered, and even to *abhor*, to have horror of something. All these connotations would suit *Inferno* XXV, but of course Dante himself should have the last word. And he uses 'abborra' again in *Inferno* XXXI, in Virgil's reply to his bewildered question, 'Maestro, dì, che terra è questa?' ['Master, tell me, what city is this?'], provoked by the unusual sight of 'towers' which turn out to be the Giants. Virgil answers: 'Però che tu trascorri | per le tenebre troppo da la lungi, | avvien che poi nel maginare abborri': you are confused in imagining because you pass through the darkness with your gaze from too far away. Indeed, Dante's eyes are 'confusi alquanto' at the sight of the changing and interchanging in the seventh bolgia, as he himself confesses immediately after presenting his excuses for writing with a faulty pen.

Confusion: a state of bewilderment, of 'smarrimento'. And the pilgrim has good reason to be bewildered, given the fusing of shapes, con-fusion, which the poet has set out before him. He states that his spirit was, at the sight of all this, 'smagato', overwhelmed. Elsewhere in the *Commedia* 'smagare' and 'dismagare' have the sense of diminishing or removing. Haste 'dismaga', diminishes, the dignity and decorum of any action. Engrossed in the contemplation which she symbolizes, Rachel never deflects her gaze from the mirror, 'mai non si smaga | dal suo miraglio', which is Aristotle's 'contemplation of contemplation' and coincides with the highest levels of Christian mysticism. Dante himself exhorts the reader not to wander from good intentions of conversion even though disheartened by the suffering of the proud: 'Non vo' però, lettor, che tu ti smaghi | di buon proponimento' ['But I would not have you, reader, fall away from good resolve'].[59] While in *Vita Nuova* and *Rime* 'smagare' often means 'to bewilder', 'to lose',[60] there are two points in the *Commedia* which interest us more closely here. In *Purgatorio* XIX, the woman who appears to Dante in a dream sings 'Io son ... io son dolce serena, | che' marinari in mezzo mar dismago' ['I am the sweet siren who beguile the sailors in mid-sea'], recreating in one stroke the whole incantation which the Sirens exercise on sailors (and on Ulysses, who is evoked immediately afterwards). In *Paradiso* III, the pilgrim catches sight of a shade more desirous than the others to speak to him. He turns towards her to question her 'quasi com'uom cui troppa voglia smaga' ['all but overcome with excess of eagerness'].[61] That shade reveals itself shortly afterwards — and here we are finally back with the Donati family — as Piccarda, sister of Forese and Corso, niece of Buoso the thief.

Smagare: the two extremes of *smarrimento*, being overwhelmed, in Hell and in Paradise, the first produced by anguish, the second by overly intense desire. Almost, in each case, a fainting, a loss of the senses. This is the effect which the metamorphic punishments in *Inferno* XXV have on Dante — the confusion produced by the uncanny. That the poet is using it to entrance and unnerve us, to keep us from straying from good intentions is demonstrated throughout the canto. Dante speaks elsewhere of the wonder and stupor which love of wisdom arouses in him and which his poetry aims to bring out in us. Shortly, in the circle of traitors, he will use pure horror.[62] Here, he wants to render us powerless, lead us to bewilderment, as though bringing us closer to that perdition beyond which are the thieves, their original image cancelled forever, one face alone now containing two lost souls, the human and divine likenesses completely perverted. He has created hypnotic poetry, as though inducing us to yawn from drowsiness or fever. He has exerted a kind of magic. He has 'smagato' his readers, distressed and overwhelmed them, building a poetry and a poetics of *dismay*.

II

RECOGNITION AND POETRY: FORESE

When Dante places members of the Donati family on stage in the *Commedia*, he introduces certain features common to all the scenes. First, there is, to varying degrees, the theme of transformation, as if inspired by the mutations, degeneration, and strife of the great Florentine families discussed by Cacciaguida (who mentions Ubertino and Gualdrada Donati) in *Paradiso* XVI: the thieves' 'change and interchange', the 'counterfeiting' of Buoso Donati, the 'changed features' of Forese, the 'transmutation' of Piccarda from 'former knowledge' thanks to the 'I know not what of divine' which shines forth from her appearance. Secondly, we encounter highly skilful dramatic devices: the transformations of the thieves are part of the intricate mechanism of *Inferno* XXIV–XXV; the conversation with Forese leads to the one with Bonagiunta da Lucca and continues after it: within that conversation, Dante's question about Piccarda and the prophecy of Corso's death and damnation are highlighted; the meeting with Piccarda provides the cue for introducing Constance. Chinese boxes and mirroring structures dominate the episodes, whose extent and all-inclusive potentialities constitute further proof of Dante's attention to the Donati.[63]

The episodes where brother and sister, Forese and Piccarda, appear on the scene share the dramatic development of recognition, already touched upon, as if literally 'by … chance', in *Inferno* XXV. In both cases, this is linked to the theme of transformation which both characters undergo: by Forese, repenting for his gluttony, now presented as a mere skull, a soul 'dark and hollow in the eyes, pallid in face' and so scrawny that skin clings to his bones; by Piccarda, who on the other hand, thanks to her blessed state, has become 'more beautiful'. In both theatre and fiction, recognition always marks a moment of intense emotion, but also of supreme gnoseological value: within it a human being's recovery of knowledge brings with it the discovery of new knowledge, the deepening of self-awareness and everything that is already known.[64] As he shows in the scenes with Virgil and Brunetto in *Inferno* I and XV, with Statius in *Purgatorio* XXI–XXII, and with Beatrice in *Purgatorio* XXX, Dante can manoeuvre these aspects of recognition with consummate skill.[65] And in the case of Forese, with phenomenal orchestration.

✻   ✻   ✻

When Virgil, Statius, and Dante reach the sixth terrace of Purgatory — the first two in front, the third 'soletto di retro', by himself, behind the other two, intent on listening to their talk which 'a poetar' gives him 'intelletto', 'understanding in making verse' — the scene is in the first instance dominated by a tree laden with 'fruits that smelled sweet and good' and whose leaves are dripping with clear water. From its branches comes a voice which, following God's warning in Genesis,[66] calls out 'Di questo cibo avrete caro' ['you may not eat of this food'], announcing a series of examples of temperance. While Dante strains his eyes to gaze inside the branches 'as he sometimes does who wastes his life after the birds', Virgil encourages him to continue with his journey. 'Ed ecco' ['And lo'], we hear simultaneous crying and singing, in tones which bring both pleasure and pain, verse 17 of the *Miserere*, Psalm 50, 'Labia mea, Domine': 'O Lord, open thou my lips, and my mouth shall shew forth thy praise'. The biblical formula 'And lo' marks the start of an extraordinary scene.[67] Surprised by the singing, Dante asks Virgil what it is that he hears. Virgil replies by using for the first time words repeated so often in these two cantos of *Purgatorio*, 'ombre' and 'nodo', and which will recur at a crucial point in canto XXIV: 'Ombre che vanno | forse di lor dover solvendo il nodo': 'Shades perhaps untying the knot of their debt' towards God by purging their gluttony.

The voices dominating the initial lines of canto XXIII thus become shades, and immediately throng in a procession of souls who move along swiftly though absorbed in thought and wonder. Like self-absorbed pilgrims who, on meeting a stranger, turn towards him without stopping, so now, says Dante, a 'turba tacita e devota' ['a crowd of souls, silent and devout'] overtakes the three poets, and gazes at them in bewilderment. In the silence following the singing of the *Miserere* the meditative and light-passing spirits form a spectral vision:

> Ne li occhi era ciascuna oscura e cava,
> pallida ne la faccia, e tanto scema
> che da l'ossa la pelle s'informava.
>
> [Each was dark and hollow in the eyes,
> pallid in face, and so wasted
> that the skin took shape from the bones.]

Definitely shades, now: skeletal ghosts, whose dark, deep-ringed eyes are the only things visible in waxy faces, whose skin has no shape but the bone beneath it. Dante the poet, who is not lacking powerful biblical examples,[68] comments that not even Ovid's Erisychthon, condemned to such insatiable hunger that he gnawed his own flesh, became so 'withered to the very rind'. Dante the character, however, is thinking not only of the classical myth but also of the time when the Jews lost Jerusalem by giving themselves up to the Romans on account of their hunger and Mary of Eleazarus 'nel figlio diè di becco', bit and ate the flesh of her child:[69] a terrifying pairing of allusions, which calls to mind Ugolino's 'fasting'.[70] But Dante insists once more: returning to the dark and sunken eyes he has just described, he now shows us circles which look like 'rings with no gems', that eye-sockets that seem empty. Those, he adds, who read the word 'omo' in men's faces, where the two *O* shapes are the eyes and the *M* the shape made by the nose, cheekbones and curve of the eyebrows, would easily recognize the *M*. Faces reduced to letters: and pre-eminent amongst them are the bony sockets which once again cancel out the pupils of the eyes. How meaningless this 'recognition' is! It seems mere reading, and not even of a whole word but just one letter. Of course, notes the poet, no one would believe that the mere smell alone of fruit and water could produce such an effect simply by generating the desire to eat and drink: no one, at least, who does not know how this occurs in souls without bodies. With a brief 'aside', to which he returns immediately afterwards when he declares his own astonishment in contemplating the cause of such hunger, Dante prepares for his magisterial invention of canto XXV.

At the same time, he continues to emphasize these spirits' terminal consumption, their 'leanness' and 'wretched scurf'. As though gouging it out of their empty eye-sockets, Dante makes true recognition emerge from them, projecting the moment forward, holding it for two lines, and finally concentrating it in a steady gaze, which suddenly reacquires eyes as though making them rise from some indeterminate depths of the skull. '*Già era* in ammirar che sì li affama' ['*I was now* wondering what so famishes them'], he writes, echoing once more the narrative mode of Scripture, '*ed ecco* del profondo de la testa | volse a me li occhi un'ombra e guardò fiso' ['*when lo*, from the depth of the head a shade turned his eyes on me and looked steadily']. The crowd of shades becomes one shade, *this one*, and the 'omo' takes on the appearance of a man turning his eyes towards his fellow man. Here, *he* is the first to recognize, and, just as Brunetto Latini exclaimed 'Qual maraviglia!' in *Inferno* XV,[71] so this shade cries out, with the variation in the word used enabling us to see the abyss between Hell and Purgatory, 'Qual *grazia* m'è questa?'. Dante takes his time, however: he takes two *terzine* before exploding the agnition in the last word of the second. The face alone would never have been enough for the recognition: it is the voice, the unique part of a person's identity, which reveals what appearance has destroyed. This is the spark which rekindles knowledge, which illuminates the 'changed features'. So now at last Dante recognizes the face of Forese:

> Mai non l'avrei riconosciuto al viso;
> ma ne la voce sua mi fu palese
> ciò che l'aspetto in sé avea conquiso.
> Questa favilla tutta mi raccese
> mia conoscenza a la cangiata labbia,
> e ravvisai la faccia di Forese.
>
> [I should never have known him again by his looks,
> but in his voice was plain to me
> that which was destroyed in his aspect;
> that spark rekindled in me
> all my knowledge of the changed features
> and I recognized the face of Forese.]

The name is the definitive seal: but before reaching it we pass twice from ignorance to knowledge, as if pacing out the whole process again, savouring it fully in the retarding of the lines: from 'mai non l'avrei riconosciuto' to 'mi fu palese', from 'tutta mi raccese mia conoscenza' to 'ravvisai'; from an unknown face to *his*, familiar, voice, through the disfigured and emaciated shape; and again from the voice which is now 'favilla', through the 'cangiata labbia', to the face of his friend.[72]

The voice is the sign which triggers memory, as will happen six centuries later for Marcel in the boyish laughter of his schoolmate during the *matinée* at the Guermantes.[73] But in Dante the mechanism has a rather special brightness and ardour: the sign is a language, a spark which kindles knowledge, and this appears as a full fire, illuminating by reflection the face perceived. A face: for apart from this we shall see nothing of Forese. And yet this is enough, shining like a light: because in a face, as Dante says in the *Convivio*, 'l'ultima potenza de la materia, la quale è in tutti dissimile, ... si riduce in atto' ['the ultimate potency of matter, different in each person ... is enacted']. Indeed the face gathers together all the main senses — sight, taste, smell, and hearing — and so 'the soul is manifest therein and operates with a more subtle craft'. The 'ultimate potency of matter' is actuated in the human face, where 'the soul-form operates better'.[74]

It is thus the very essence of Forese that is revealed to Dante here, the union within him of matter and form, body and soul. And while the means of this fusion which takes place in the shade is to be the subject of Statius' marvellous exposition in canto XXV, it will suffice to set it against the apparently nominal general essence grasped earlier ('omo') to understand how substantial and individual it appears here: like Aristotle's *tode ti*, the universal which is actuated in the particular, the 'quod quid est', or 'quidditas', of the Scholastics.

∗ ∗ ∗

Forese's surprise is shown in his exultation, for meeting Dante in the afterlife seems to him like a true miracle, a 'grazia' from above. It quickly, however, becomes self-awareness and desire to learn what has happened to his friend. What now prevails is his awareness of his condition and appearance. As Forese tells Dante, referring to the 'wretched scurf' and 'leanness' of all his companions, he is no more than the 'asciutta scabbia', the 'withered scab' that discolours his skin, a 'lack of flesh': but still a person, now wishing urgently and passionately to rekindle past bonds, imploring Dante — 'tell me the truth about yourself' — not to stand there without speaking to him but to identify the two souls who are his companions.

In Aristotle, recognition 'is a passage from not knowing to knowing which produces friendship or enmity',[75] and in *Purgatorio* XXIII it fully reveals *philia*, a core dimension of human relations, in which 'si fa uno di più' and which has for Dante, as for Aristotle, a highly ethical value, since it is necessary for the 'vita perfetta':[76] that friendship between the two which had been and continues to be their bond. Nor should one forget that *Purgatorio*, beginning with the Casella episode, is the *cantica* of friendship.

In the light of this feeling, the remembrance of things past now begins. Without answering Forese's question, caught up in his own astonishment and desire to know, Dante asks him a question of his own, with the same pathos that pervades his friend's voice:

> Però mi dì, per Dio, che sì vi sfoglia;
> non mi far dir mentr'io mi maraviglio,
> ché mai può dir chi è pien d'altra voglia.
>
> [Therefore tell me, in God's name, what so wastes you.
> Do not make me speak while I am marvelling,
> For he can ill speak whose mind is full of something else.]

Dante returns to the question tormenting him, to the nature of this extreme emaciation which strips away leaf after leaf, layer after layer of flesh (or parchment where the word 'omo' is written). But in questioning his friend he evokes the past and links it to the present he reads in his face, already wept over in the supreme moment of his death and which now appears so disfigured.[77] Forese replies by explaining the divine origin of the purification to which all sinners of gluttony are subjected, claiming that their punishment is sanctification and their suffering more like solace, for the desire ('voglia') that urges them towards the trees is the same penance for their sins as that which led Christ on the cross to call out gladly ('lieto') 'Eli, Eli lama sabachthani?'.

An extraordinarily paradoxical comparison, if one believes that Jesus' last words as reported by Mark and Matthew, 'My God, my God, why hast thou forsaken me?', are dictated by despair rather than joy, yet appropriate in the theological and poetic plot of *Purgatorio* XXIII, where the 'grace' that Forese feels on seeing Dante seems to become the 'voglia' of purification, the same that dominates the Redeemer's sacrifice. As he has already done for theft in *Inferno* XXV, Dante the architect thus sets the sin of gluttony — and its purgatorial redemption[78] — within the general history of salvation, linking in a grand biblical arch, from the Fall in Genesis to the Passion and Redemption, and back to the Fall,[79] that daily sin whose primeval antecedent was identified by theological tradition as, simultaneously, gluttony, pride, and avarice.[80]

While Forese thus seems to take on, obliquely, a passing resemblance to the crucified Christ, Dante the character cannot shift his attention away from what is really troubling him: the death of his friend. Less than five years have passed, he tells him, 'da quel dì | nel qual mutasti mondo a miglior vita' ['since that day when you exchanged worlds for a better life']: the burning awareness of death ('la faccia tua, ch'io lagrimai già morta'), while still tinged with grief for the past, is attenuated by the recognition that it also announces a 'better life': that Forese has survived death and achieved eternal life. These are the two hopes that Christianity offers to believers. And recognition, which previously only meant passing from ignorance to knowledge, and then pointed to *philia*, is now complete, focusing, as in Aristotle's definition, on the 'fortune', the *eutykhia* of its protagonist.[81] In this lies the subtle distinction between the acts of agnition regarding Brunetto and Forese: while the former has taught Dante 'how man makes himself eternal', and believes he is still living in his *Trésor* while in fact he has obtained a terminal *dystykhia* on account of his sodomy, the latter repented his gluttony on the point of death, thus achieving *eutykhia*, a happy destiny.

But Dante is not content with this. He wants to know how Forese managed to reach Purgatory Proper since he died fewer than five years earlier: if he repented only at the end, he should still be in Antepurgatory 'where time is redeemed by time'. The poet answers his own question with a stroke of genius. It was, Forese claims, his wife, 'la Nella mia', who 'con suo pianger dirotto' ['by her flood of tears'] helped him to obtain the bitter-sweet suffering of purgatory. With her devout prayers and sighs, she obtained a shortening of his purification. Forese's gratitude is profound recognition, vibrant with affection: dominating it is his love for his wife, God's love for her (to the extent that Nella takes on the features of a Beatrice, a Lucy, a Mary), and her 'bene operare', the incarnation of true ethical virtue:[82]

> Tanto è a Dio più cara e più diletta
> la vedovella mia, che molto amai,
> quanto in bene operare è più soletta …
>
> [So much more precious to God and more beloved
> is my widow, whom I greatly loved,
> as she is more alone in well-doing …]

After Forese's violent prophetic invective against the degenerate Florentine women which starts with his mention of Nella's solitude in barbarian Florence,[83] he turns to Dante to ask him about himself and the two shades accompanying him. Dante replies with a double movement which reflects once again the scene with Brunetto, returning to the remembrance of things past and focusing decisively on times present.[84] Even fuller recognition takes shape through his words, touching the very life of each of them and the memory which in the present retraces the past:

> Per ch'io a lui: 'Se tu riduci a mente
> qual fosti meco, e qual io teco fui,
> ancor fia grave il memorar presente …'

> [Whereupon I said to him: 'If you bring back to mind
> what you were with me and I with you,
> the present memory will be grievous still …']

On the one hand there is the memory of the past relationship ('qual fosti meco, e qual io teco fui'), on the other the remembering, now, of that same period ('il memorar presente'), which accomplishes the former through suffering ('fia grave'). There is a substantial difference between the two types of memory, which Aristotle called *mneme* and *anamnesis* and Thomas Aquinas *memorari* and *reminisci*, and which can be rendered as 'memory' and 'reminiscence'. The first, the Scholastic *memorari*, 'is nothing other than preserving well what has been acquired', while the second, *reminisci*, is 'a finding again (*reinventio*) of what was once acquired but not well preserved'.[85] Memory comes before reminiscence and is common to animals as well as to humankind; reminiscence belongs only to humanity, and implies the intervention of will: 'it is a kind of inference' (*syllogismus*) and 'a kind of search' (*inquisitio*), for 'he who remembers fixes by inference that which he has seen or heard or experienced'.[86] Aristotle criticizes Plato's theory according to which 'learning is reminiscence': 'fore-knowledge of a single object can never occur', he claims; 'rather, while induction is developing, we take on the knowledge of particular objects *as though we recognized them*'.[87] Reminiscence is for him a process of gaining awareness.

It is this type of memory and knowledge that Dante explores in the recognition with Forese, giving it all the pathos of a process which concerns not just any object or scientific data, but a person in the flesh and above all in the bone. Dante knows that the 'memorar presente' (in which the *memorari* of Aquinas seems to echo) will become 'grievous' when Forese has recalled the relationship they had, that is when he has accomplished an operation of *reminisci* in which his will plays a part (and to that *deliberativum* he invites his friend with 'se tu riduci a mente', 'if you bring back to mind'). *Purgatorio* XXIII, like *Inferno* XV, makes poetry out of memory, and relies, like Proust's *Recherche*, on a poetics of *reminiscence*.

*   *   *

Forese and Dante must rediscover the past, employing *reinventio*. It seems beyond any doubt that the famous *tenzone* plays a major role here.[88] Without it, this passage from *Purgatorio* would make no sense, whereas it has a number of links with cantos XXIII–XXIV, from the accusation of gluttony to verbal repetition.[89] It is also worth pointing out that while the *tenzone* describes a nocturnal journey by Forese towards the 'ditches' of the dead and the 'knot' that ties Alighiero, Dante's father,[90] Dante replies to his friend, in canto XXIII, with an account of his journey among the dead (the initial formula is similar: 'l'altra notte', 'l'altr'ier')[91] as far as these shades 'who perhaps go loosing the knot of their debt', and, in the next canto, as far as the 'knot' that kept

Bonagiunta, Jacopo da Lentini, and Guittone d'Arezzo 'on this side of the *dolce stil novo*'.[92]

In the *tenzone*, that 'ill-fated wife of Bicci, known to us as Forese', who coughs with the cold because she has too few blankets on her bed, and also an impotent husband ('copertoio … cortonese'), harbours 'bad wishes' ('mala voglia'),[93] and feels 'a lack in her nest' ('difetto al nido'), whereas in the *Commedia*, in perfect counterpoint, Nella is an example of 'well-doing' and the object of her husband's great love. The 'altra mala voglia' of which Dante accuses his friend's wife in the first of his sonnets becomes the 'altra voglia', the pilgrim's own curiosity, in the purgatorial encounter. Forese's 'faccia fessa' in the *tenzone* returns as a 'disfigured' face in *Purgatorio*.[94] The accusation of thieving which Dante levelled at his friend and at the whole Donati family is repeated in *Inferno* XXV (and perhaps in the 'other circles' where Forese should have done penance for his other sins). And finally, in the Middle Ages from Gregory the Great to Thomas, the 'daughters' of gluttony are seen as *immunditia* or impurity as regards the body, and, as regards the soul, *hebetudo sensus circa intelligentiam, inepta laetitia, multiloquium* and *scurrilitas*:[95] a dulling which the sense operates upon intelligence, foolhardy cheerfulness, gossip, and scurrility, 'that is, a certain buffoonery in external gestures': all vices which match perfectly the context of the *tenzone* and for which Forese and Dante are now paying, the former through purgatorial purification, the latter by staging this conversation with his friend.

There is undoubtedly a relationship between 'Forese's empirically verifiable and verified gluttony' and the 'verbal and stylistic gluttony, of a baser species, which the sonnets reveal'.[96] Just as a close relationship exists between 'a phase of existence, now held as "grievous" by memory and repudiated', 'a phase of intellectual, and more specifically poetic, activity, felt to be a more lowly thing of the past', and 'the phase of the "realistic", or more specifically "comic", rhymes, as those of the *tenzone*'.[97] For in the final analysis it is his own intellectual and poetic journey that Dante 're-cognizes' in these cantos of *Purgatorio* and in the multilayered fabric into which they are woven: from the 'dear and kindly paternal image' of Brunetto, Forese's infernal counterpoint, to Forese himself, who had taken part in a playful contest with Dante, from Bonagiunta, Guittone, and Jacopo da Lentini in canto XXIV to Guinizzelli and Arnaut in canto XXVI.[98]

Dante's meditation on poetry, which seems to begin with the entrance into the sixth terrace, when the conversation between Virgil and Statius gives him 'understanding in making verse', in fact opens with the appearance of Statius and the scene of recognition between him and Virgil in canto XXI. It continues in the following canto with the detour into Limbo where Statius lists the authors and mythological characters not contemplated in *Inferno* IV. This is a meditation on the classical antecedents which throng around the 'company of six' in the first circle of Hell, and on the complex relations of paternity, maternity, and filial relations in literature and in eternal destiny (Statius-Virgil). The Forese–Bonagiunta–Guinizzelli–Arnaut sequence is a review and recognition of Dante's poetical experiences in the vernacular: where the Forese episode frames the scene with Bonagiunta, leading into it and mingling with it (the recognition of the one is a prelude to recognizing the other: 'what a favour is this to me!', 'but tell me if I see here'), and the conversation with Bonagiunta then opens the way for the meeting with Guinizzelli and Arnaut.

Of course, in order to measure Dante's path from the *tenzone* to the *Commedia*, and more specifically, beyond that other 'tenzone' which is the dispute between Sinon and Master Adam in *Inferno* XXX, to the *Purgatorio*, it would be enough to read aloud, one after the other, *Chi udisse tossir* and the passage in canto XXIII in which Forese speaks about Nella, or *L'altra notte mi venne* and the passage from *Purgatorio* XXIII in which Dante re-evokes for his friend his own otherworldly journey of salvation from Hell to Purgatory, from Virgil to Beatrice — or simply to compare Dante's use of the word 'carne' in his second sonnet of the *tenzone* and in *Purgatorio* XXIII:

> Ben ti faranno il nodo Salomone,
> Bicci novello, e' petti de le starne,
> ma peggio fia la lonza del castrone,
> ché 'l cuoio farà vendetta de la carne.
>
> [Partridge breasts, young Bicci,
> will truss you in Solomon's knot all right!
> But loins of mutton will be still worse for you,
> for the skin will take revenge for the flesh!][99]

> '... Di quella vita mi volse costui
> che mi va innanzi, l'altr'ier, quando tonda
> vi si mostrò la suora di colui',
>   e 'l sol mostrai; 'costui per la profonda
> notte menato m'ha de' veri morti
> con questa vera carne che 'l seconda ...'
>
> ['... He that goes before me turned me
> from that life some days ago, when
> the sister of him' — and I pointed to the sun —
> 'showed herself round to you.
> It is he who has led me through the profound
> night of the truly dead with this true flesh that follows him ...']

The 'carne' of the sonnet is located between the butcher's shop, in which partridge breasts and mutton chops are laid out, and the tannery, where animal hide is turned into parchment to be used by Forese in recording his debts. It is a good example of fierce realism and at the same time of *trobar clus*[100] — in short, of perfect 'poesia giocosa'. Metaphorically, it is also a precise and cruel description of Forese's punishment in Purgatory, where the withered and flaking skin of the sinner will take its revenge on the flesh, for the meat which Forese consumed in abundance, and for gluttony which is by definition of the flesh: is he not also reduced to 'a lack of flesh', to a 'difetto de la carne'? The passage in *Purgatorio*, on the other hand, presents no obscure game, but a plain and simple discourse in which the word 'carne' acquires strength from its attribute 'vera', denoting the actual body with which Dante, to the astonishment of the souls, passes through the other world. It stands out all the more in opposition to the 'veri morti' — the damned, dead in body and spirit — through whose deep night Virgil has led the pilgrim. Truly dead, real flesh: not mere realism, but two simple, formidable truths.

Against the fracture which Dante establishes in his own poetic experience between the *tenzone* and *Purgatorio*, the continuity between the Stilnovo and the *Commedia* indicated in his meeting with Bonagiunta stands out. When Bonagiunta asks him if he really is the man who 'brought forth the new rhymes, beginning with *Donne ch'avete intelletto d'amore*', Dante replies using not the past, but the present tense:[101] 'I' mi *son* un che, quando | Amor mi spira, *noto*, e a quel modo ch'e' ditta dentro *vo* significando' ['I *am* one who, when love breathes in me, *take* note, and in that manner which he dictates within *go* setting it forth']. The sentence links the *Vita nuova* and the *Commedia*: the announcement, in the former, of the poetry of 'praise', which is a new 'cominciamento' for the tongue that 'spoke almost as though moving by itself',[102] and the full accomplishment of the latter in 'notation' inspired by Love. Dante makes this statement in the presence not only of Bonagiunta but also of Forese (to whom he has already mentioned Beatrice) and Statius, who has declared his love towards Virgil. Later, Piccarda will extol charity and will seem to be 'burning with love in the first fire'. Dante's poetry is both love poetry and a poetry of love.

All this continuity is visible, so to speak, in the alternation of small letters ('amore' in *Donne ch'avete*) and capitals ('Amore' in *Purgatorio* XXIV). This includes the dimension of profane Love (often with a capital letter, as personification, in *Vita nuova*) and sacred, or rather divine Love (the Spirit) which, like a new Bible, 'inspires' and dictates the *Commedia*.[103] The opening of St Ivo's *Epistle to Severinus on Charity*, from which Dante's formulation seems to derive, also alternates 'amor' and 'charitas',[104] while the striking novelty of the poem is signalled by the *incipit* of Dante's reply to Bonagiunta, 'I' mi son un', 'I am one'. What resonates here is not so much the echo of the tautological divine proclamation in Exodus, 'Ego sum qui sum', which would cast a shadow of Luciferine presumption upon Dante, but his apostolic, Pauline version, 'sum id quod sum'. It is in fact to Paul that Dante compares himself in *Inferno* II, and Paul whom he cites at the beginning of *Paradiso* for his own ascent.[105]

∗   ∗   ∗

The recognition in cantos XXIII–XXIV of *Purgatorio* opens the way to all this. It is a highly dramatic recognition of death and the essence of mankind, sin and suffering, past life and literature. Dante invents for it a poetry and a poetics of the shade which fills cantos XXI to XXVI of *Purgatorio*, from the moment in which Statius appears on the scene until Guido Guinizzelli separates himself from the throng of the lustful in *Purgatorio* XXVI.[106] After the initial cantos of *Inferno*, these are the cantos in which the word 'ombra' appears most frequently of all throughout the poem. The first examples demonstrate this, when Virgil says to Statius, who has bent down to embrace his feet as a mark of veneration, 'Frate, | non far, ché tu se' ombra e ombra vedi' ['Brother, do not so, for you are a shade and a shade you see'], and when Statius, getting up immediately, replies:

> Or puoi la quantitate
> comprender de l'amor che a te mi scalda,
> quand'io dismento nostra vanitate,
>   trattando l'ombre come cosa salda.

> [Now you can understand the measure
> of the love that burns in me for you,
> when I forget our emptiness
> and treat shades as solid things.]

To treat the shades as 'solid things' is already, for the author of the *Commedia*, a literary project: it means imagining and describing the spirits of the other world as though they had a reality not ascribed to them in the classical tradition from Homer to Virgil.[107] And while Dante had indicated the 'vanità che par persona' ['the emptiness that seems a real body'] of the gluttons of Hell, more unfortunate relatives and hardened sinners,[108] it is precisely between the empty and the solid that the shades of the gluttons of Purgatory are located. At the start of canto xxiv they seem to Dante to be 'cose rimorte', inert objects twice dead, but objects nevertheless: things with skulls, bones, skin, eye sockets, things that certainly have 'difetto di carne' but which suffer on account of it. What a powerful contrast there is between these shades and the shadow that Dante projects with his body! — nowhere more memorably than on entering the terrace of the lustful, when the setting sun casts white light to the west, across sky that had previously been blue, and strikes the pilgrim on the right: then, says the poet, 'io facea con l'*ombra* più rovente | parer la fiamma; e pur a tanto indizio vidi molt'*ombre*, andando, poner mente' ['with my *shadow* I made the flame appear more glowing, and even at that faint sign I saw many of the *shades*, as they went, give heed']. The shadow cast by Dante's body makes the wall of flame which surrounds the entire terrace appear even redder, because it intercepts the light of the setting sun: as the shades are quick to point out, Dante has no 'corpo fittizio', but 'vera carne'.

The reader who has followed the poet up to this point will realize what he means by 'corpo fittizio'. Several hints from the Forese canto onwards have announced the explanation offered by Statius in *Purgatorio* xxv. No shade can confer greater urgency on the problem than Forese, who is so close to Dante and so emaciated.[109] No one is fitter to solving it than Statius, a shade who wishes to embrace the feet of another shade. Without repeating Statius's exposition here,[110] I simply wish to point out that it sketches a physiology, a metaphysics, and a poetics of the shade. In the first place, it clarifies what appeared to be a true mystery at the beginning of *Purgatorio*, where Virgil proclaimed that the shades of the afterlife have the same ethereal substance as the transparent heavens:[111] it is the Power of God which makes these diaphanous bodies capable of 'suffering torments of heat and frost', and He does not want the 'how' to be revealed to us.[112] Secondly, the entirely rational explanation offered by Statius[113] delineates a formidable continuity from body to soul and on to the transient body of the afterlife, from the formation of the human embryo to the infusion of the divine spirit into it, and the survival of the soul after death, to the extent that the soul cannot avoid giving birth to a sort of second body, the aerial one of the shade. Dominating the entire process is 'formative virtue', from the time when the pure blood flows to the heart and then descends as sperm 'ov'è più bello | tacer che dire', to the instant at which the soul, after death, 'radiates round about, in form and measure as in the living members', just as it did in giving life to the organs of the first body. The 'virtù formativa' does not cease with death, since it is of the soul, which survives. And the soul is located at the centre of the whole metamorphosis which a human being undergoes after the end of the body.[114] It is made more powerful after death: while the bodily faculties are indeed now 'mute', the spiritual ones — memory, intelligence, and will — become 'in atto molto più che prima agute'. The 'shade' of the afterlife is such, and is so called, precisely because that body has a visible appearance, a 'paruta' or 'semblance', possessed by the shadow of earthly bodies: 'it has their form, but not their consistency'.[115] It is the shade which forms the organs of each sense, but the soul remains none the less the source of passions and their expression. Inverting the sense of a passage from the *Aeneid*, Dante says 'by this we speak and by this we smile, by this we shed tears and make sighs'.[116] The shade thus shapes itself according to the various feelings of the soul: 'secondo che ci affliggono i disiri | e li altri affetti, l'ombra si figura'.

A mystery, yet a natural process: this is the nature of shade-formation with which Dante replies to centuries, if not millennia, of debate on the survival of a bodily entity after death. For him, truth lies in the spirit's union with some corporeal shape (it is, after all, the truth proclaimed by the incarnation and then the resurrection of Christ). The Dantean shade therefore lies between the earthly human being, in whom body and soul are united, and the human person as will be resurrected on the last day, once again perfect and whole[117] — a state of transition between the flesh of yesterday and the mysterious body of tomorrow. It is both the fulfilment of the human being of this world and a prefiguring of the human being which is to come after the day of Judgement: and thus, in this second sense, shade, actual *umbra* in the figural sense of the term.[118] This appears all the more real in Purgatory, the transitional kingdom *par excellence*. It is, of course, significant that the explanation is entrusted to Statius, who has terminated his purification and is rising towards his ultimate goal, Paradise. It will come, then, as no surprise that towards the end of *Purgatorio*, when for the first time the unveiling of Beatrice's mouth reveals the 'splendour of living eternal light', which is the same as that of Wisdom, Dante speaks of the poet's inspiration and task as of a drinking at the Castalian spring or becoming 'pale under the *shade* of Parnassus'.[119]

The souls in Purgatory all await that accomplishment as liberation. Typological thought had meant, for St Paul, waiting for the fullness of time and the fulfilment of all in Christ.[120] Poetry of the shade means, therefore, in this case, the poetry of *attente*: of waiting, of expectancy. This is the feeling shown on a literal, dramatic level by both Forese and Dante at the end of their long conversation, the former asking 'Quando fia ch'io ti riveggia?' ['How long will it be till I see you again?'], and the second replying 'I know not how long I shall live; but truly my return will not be so soon that in desire I shall not be sooner at the shore'. This is also what pervades the close of canto xxiv, where Dante feels a breeze upon his face as '*herald* of the dawn': 'quale, *annunziatrice* de li albori, | l'aura di maggio movesi e olezza'. The breeze is in fact produced by the wing of the angel which cancels another *P* from his brow and spreads the perfume of ambrosia, a divine fragrance. It is this same angel who brings the canto to a close, raising against gluttony an evangelical beatitude which exalts waiting and accomplishment: 'Blessed are they which do hunger and thirst after righteousness: for they shall be filled'. At the opening of the canto, Dante had asked Forese for news of his sister Piccarda. He is already waiting to meet her. But for Piccarda Donati, who will also appear as a shade, the only waiting is for resurrection: 'bella' and 'buona', 'fair' and 'good' during her earthly life, 'she already triumphs in high Olympus, rejoicing in her crown', as Forese reveals to Dante. And at the end of Purgatorio xxiv, it is towards the peace celebrated by Piccarda that the angel points the way.[121]

III
PEACE AND THE MIND IN LOVE: PICCARDA

To avoid lingering in Antepurgatory, the Donati require the prayers of a woman, Forese's wife Nella. Only a woman, Piccarda, can place them in Paradise. But in order to reach Paradise, the Donati must abandon the earthly world: as Piccarda says, in order to follow St Clare and her teaching, 'Dal mondo … giovinetta fuggi'mi', she fled from the world as a young girl. She chose 'closure' — the cloister and *clausura* — against earthly joys and torments: 'nel suo abito mi chiusi', by wrapping herself in St Clare's habit. But even in Paradise the worldly deeds of the Donati continue to be reflected, as though history were tormenting them there too. The 'tela', the web which Dante questions Piccarda about, is the story of why she 'non trasse infino a co la spola' ['did not draw the shuttle to the end'], that is, did not weave the yarn of her monastic vow to the utmost by fulfilling it throughout her existence. It is a 'web' of violence and abuse through which the world bursts in on the 'dolce chiostra', snatching Piccarda from God. After promising herself to Him in eternal vows and taking Constance as her name, she had been forced by her brother Corso to marry Rossellino della Tosa[122] and destined to a life which, as she tells us with marvellously painful reticence from her place in Paradise, was known only to the Lord:

> Uomini poi, a mal più ch'a bene usi,
> fuor mi rapiron de la dolce chiostra:
> Iddio si sa qual poi mia vita fusi.
>
> [Then men more used to evil than to good
> snatched me from the sweet cloister.
> God knows what my life then became.]

Men: no name or kinship is mentioned, simply the male gender which has identified the Donati from Hell to Purgatory. The first canto of *Paradiso* in which souls appear is, on the other hand, completely female: from Beatrice to Piccarda, St Clare, and Constance, and back to Beatrice. Women are the first annunciation of Paradise Proper. As if to emphasize the honour, the architect of the *Commedia* clarifies one central dynamic: Piccarda and Constance are indeed relegated to this first Heaven of the Moon 'through neglect of vows',[123] but, as the following canto explains, not because this sphere is assigned to them as the seat of their blessed life, but to signify to us concretely and comprehensibly the level they occupy in the real paradise, the Empyrean.[124] 'Ogne dove / in cielo è paradiso' ['Everywhere in heaven is Paradise'], Dante realizes, '*etsi* la grazia / del sommo ben d'un modo non vi piove' ['even though the grace of the Supreme Good does not rain there in one measure']. Moreover, while Piccarda and Constance belong to the 'spera più tarda' [the slowest sphere], Beatrice and St Clare are among the higher ones, and thus the relative female fragility indicated by the worldly experiences and place in Heaven of the first two is perfectly balanced by the sublimation of Beatrice and Clare's 'perfetta vita' and 'alto merto'. In a world in which men act 'more accustomed to evil than to good' Clare's worthiness is a model for earthly life, a foreshadowing of life in Heaven, in which one wakes and sleeps until death 'with that Bridegroom' (Christ, the exact opposite of men such as Rossellino della Tosa) 'who accepts every vow that charity conforms to His pleasure'.[125]

Before Piccarda, Clare, and Constance come on the scene, Beatrice opens the third canto of *Paradiso*, the very first line immediately taking her back to Dante's past, to that love which had bonded him to her since his boyhood and which seemed to be recalled simply upon the mention of her name at the end of the first part of his conversation with Forese in *Purgatorio* XXIII.[126] Beatrice is 'that sun which first warmed my breast with love': the theme of the poetry evoked by Dante with the shades of Forese and Bonagiunta, the object of the 'nove rime'. The whole of *Paradiso* III is interwoven with echoes of Dante's poetic experience, starting from the 'dolcezza' which, according to Bonagiunta, is the distinguishing feature of the '*dolce* stil novo'.[127] When Dante addresses Piccarda as 'spirit made for bliss, who in the beams of eternal life knows the sweetness which, not tasted, never is conceived', the echo of *Tanto gentile*, of the *Vita nuova*, and even of Cavalcanti, is intentional. And in a sense one might say that the entire canto is an explication *a parte aeternitatis* of the song which Bonagiunta saw as the manifesto of the Stilnovo, *Donne ch'avete intelletto d'amore*: because the women of *Paradiso* III show full comprehension of what can now, in Heaven, be considered true love: charity directed not towards an earthly person but towards the celestial Bridegroom, God. After Dante finally recognizes Piccarda and speaks with her, that love is recalled once more, and for the second time in terms which may allude to both its divine dimension and its earthly and youthful one, the 'primo amore' of her life. Indeed, together with the other shades, Piccarda smiles at the pilgrim's question, then replies 'with such gladness that she seemed to burn in the first fire of love'.[128]

Dante proceeds by superimposition and concretion of meanings. Shortly before, Beatrice too had smiled, with burning in her eyes which now seemed 'santi'. On that occasion, Beatrice herself was described as 'dolce', but the adjective accompanied the noun 'guida'. And at the start of canto III, that sun which had warmed Dante's breast in his youth had been assigned the role of teacher: as someone who, in discussing the spots of the moon in the previous canto, had revealed to the pupil — via the method of Scholastic *quaestiones*, 'provando e riprovando' — the 'dolce aspetto' of 'bella verità' ['the sweet aspect of fair truth']. Sweetness therefore is no longer predicated only of the woman, or of what one feels when looking at her, but of her explanations and above all their content, a content which is not only true but contains a truth with the colour and appeal — evoked for the first time here in Paradise — of beauty. The young girl of Dante's first love, Beatrice has, in short, become resplendent Wisdom, bearer of Truth and Beauty. No wonder that after Piccarda has disappeared, Dante returns to Beatrice, at the end of the canto, as to an object of 'greater desire', and that in the closing lines she dazzles his sight to the point that his question is delayed, suspended in the prime moments which characterize the acquisition and action of knowledge, of wisdom: increasing desire, brightness which hinders contemplation, and new questioning.

In the scenic architecture of the canto, Beatrice none the less serves as Piccarda's midwife, while Piccarda is the first soul Dante encounters in Paradise in counterpoint to Francesca, the first shade of Hell proper, and to Pia de' Tolomei, the first female figure in Purgatory.[129] To point up the differences between them, Dante distils into his present account echoes of those two previous episodes. And he does so right from the start: for his apostrophe to the as yet unknown Piccarda, 'grazioso mi fia ...' ['it will be a kindness to me if you satisfy me with your name and with your lot'], picks up on Francesca's 'animal grazioso e benigno'; just as the 're che 'n suo voler ne 'nvoglia' [King 'who wills us to his will'], echoes the 're de l'universo' of *Inferno* v, and the 'pace' which is God's will, seen as a sea to which everything moves, is a response to the peace for which the two lovers, if they could, would pray to the Lord for Dante, while representing a counterpoint to the 'marina dove 'l Po discende | per aver pace co' seguaci sui' ['shore where the Po descends to have peace with its tributaries'] . Up to the — now sweet — 'stroke of the glottis'[130] which closes Piccarda's *recherché* 'Iddio si sa qual poi mia vita fusi' ['God knows what my life then became']: in which we find echoes of Francesca's final reticence, 'that day we read in it no farther', and above all of Pia's 'he knows of it who, first plighting troth, wedded me with his gem'.

The Francesca–Pia–Piccarda sequence outlines a most exemplary *itinerarium*: from courtly love and lust to charity (outlined with the tones of the 'cor gentile'), from a betrayed marriage to a betraying one, to marriage with the celestial Bridegroom and to that imposed by men 'more accustomed to evil than good'. In the thematic sphere of marriage, Piccarda's story and collocation link up also with those of Forese and Nella. This scene in Paradise fulfils the one in Purgatory with his friend, because Dante had asked Forese for news of his sister and Forese had told him of her triumph 'già lieta' 'ne l'alto Olimpo', but also on account of the dramatic framing of the recognition, and finally because of the shadowy consistency of the two characters' appearance. Piccarda is not a light, like the spirits who will appear in the higher Heavens, but still a shade, within which her previous features are visible.[131] This is not due to a slip on the poet's part, but for a precise reason: because, as Beatrice will explain indirectly in canto IV, on earth Piccarda lacked absolute will — the readiness for martyrdom of a Saint Lawrence or a Mucius Scaevola, and thus the perfect comprehension of divine will. In her, therefore, there remains that 'shadow of the flesh' which the Eagle of the Righteous in *Paradiso* XIX says is the mental state of those who fail to welcome the light that 'comes from the clear sky that is never clouded'.[132]

※   ※   ※

The lingering presence of the shade enables the poet to play a doubly subtle game, scenic on the one hand and thematic on the other. First, the setting. The Heaven of the Moon appears as a 'shining, dense, solid, and smooth' cloud, 'like a diamond smitten by the sun': an 'eternal pearl'[133] which receives Dante's 'transhumanized' body and Beatrice's spirit 'as water receives a ray of light and remains unbroken'.[134] The third canto of *Paradiso*, described by Tommaseo as having a 'silvery limpidness',[135] is set against this background of pearly, aquatic brightness, where the images of glass, water, and pearl construct the perfect oxymoron of the *claritas* of the shades or of the evanescence of what Beatrice calls 'vere sustanze'. The threefold simile which opens the canto scenically finds its completion only at the end, when it becomes single (only the liquid element remains of the glass, waters, and pearl), eliminating the allusion to the myth of Narcissus and the mirror,[136] and transforming the light emerging into heavy disappearing and the clear, tranquil, and shallow waters of the start into the 'acqua cupa' of the end. Shades, yes, but *clear*. 'Debili', faint too, yet visible. Not reflected images, as Dante at first believes, making the opposite mistake to that of Narcissus, but true matter, real souls. Not 'specchiati sembianti', but 'facce'. 'Vision', we might say for the first time in *Paradiso*, and here within the paradox that the shade provides, not *per speculum in aenigmate*, but *facie ad faciem*.[137] Here are the three famous opening *terzine*, and the single one that concludes the episode:

> Quali per vetri trasparenti e tersi,
> o ver per acque nitide e tranquille,
> non sì profonde che i fondi sien persi,
>   tornan di nostri visi le postille
> debili sì, che perla in bianca fronte
> non vien men tosto a le nostre pupille;
>   tali vid'io più facce a parlar pronte;
> per ch'io dentro a l'error contrario corsi
> a quel ch'accese amor tra l'omo e 'l fonte.

> [As through smooth and transparent glass,
> or through limpid and still waters
> not so deep that the bottom is lost,
> the outlines of our faces return
> so faint that a pearl on a white brow
> does not come less quickly to our eyes,
> many such faces I saw, eager to speak;
> wherefore I ran into the opposite error
> to that which kindled love between the man and the spring.]

> Così parlommi, e poi cominciò 'Ave,
> *Maria*' cantando, e cantando vanio
> come per acqua cupa cosa grave.

> [She spoke thus to me, then began singing 'Ave,
> *Maria*' and singing vanished,
> like a weight through deep water.]

Against this scenic backdrop of shade and brightness a corresponding thematic nucleus takes shape: appearing as a shade, Piccarda is entrusted with the task of expounding the way in which the 'affections' of these souls are 'solo infiammati ... nel piacer de lo Spirito Santo' ['kindled solely ... in the pleasure of the Holy Ghost'], namely in the charity which here in Paradise is devoid of shadows. Along with the *exemplum* of Constance which she points out later, Piccarda has the privilege of embodying the theme of the *more and less* which dominates the first cantos of *Paradiso*. 'The glory of Him who moves all things', the poet had proclaimed at the start of the cantica, 'penetrates the universe and shines in one part more and in another less'.[138] The problem of the unequally distributed brightness and penetration of light in the universe is what Beatrice deals with in her speech on cosmic order in canto I and when she discusses the organization of the Heavens in canto II. It is a matter of *degree*, as in the condition of Piccarda and the souls relegated to the Heaven of the Moon 'for failure in their vows'. It is the problem which Piccarda clarifies in canto III and which Beatrice picks up again and solves in cantos IV and V.

This problem dominates the scene which leads Dante, all but 'overcome with excess of eagerness', to recognize as Piccarda, whom he had asked Forese about, the shade

'most desirous of speech'. Piccarda does not reply to Dante's request by simply reveal-
ing her name and worldly condition as a 'vergine sorella', but immediately extends the
courtesy formula to the reason for her eagerness, the charity of the blessed and of God
('our charity does not shut the doors against right will, any more than His who wills
all His court to be like Himself'), and to the 'lot' which Dante takes so much to heart:
pointing out that she is blessed among the blessed 'in the slowest of the spheres',
possessing affections which rejoice because they correspond to the *order* desired by
the Spirit, and having such an apparently lowly 'lot' 'because our vows were neglected
and in some part void'. Starting from her first response, Piccarda illustrates the dual
theme: the love for, of, and within God, who governs everything in Heaven; and the
varying degrees to which human beings on earth correspond to it and to which divine
grace descends upon the blessed in Paradise.

When Dante asks her if she and the other spirits of the Moon do not desire 'a higher
place' so as to see God better and more closely and participate more in his love,
Piccarda develops her first response with her discourse on charity and beatitude
which, following Beatrice's speeches on the order of the cosmos and the Heavens, is
the third great nucleus of thought and poetry of *Paradiso*. It is charity, she says,
that 'quiets' the will of the blessed, because it makes them desire only what they have,
leaving them with no further aspiration. If they desired to be placed higher in the
Heavens, their desire would not agree with divine will which allocates them according
to varying degrees of beatitude: a thing which cannot happen in 'questi giri', where
charity is necessary, its essence consisting of the conforming of wills within the divine
will. It is in fact essential to this 'beato *esse*' [state of bliss] adds Piccarda, 'that we
keep ourselves within divine will, so that our wills are themselves made one', in such
a way that their being placed 'from height to height' through the kingdom of God is
pleasing to the whole kingdom and to the King who wills them to desire what He
wants. It is in His will that the 'peace' of the blessed dwells:

> E 'n la sua volontade è nostra pace:
> ell'è quel mare al qual tutto si move
> ciò ch'ella crïa o che natura face.

> [And in His will is our peace.
> It is that sea to which all things move,
> both what it creates and what nature makes.]

This tercet is the poetic climax of the canto, a climax which is at once ontological
and theological: it divides the universe into the product of divine creation and natural
generation, but sees it as 'tutto' and imagines this whole as moving towards the 'sea'
which is God's will and the 'gran mar de l'essere' which Beatrice spoke of at the outset
— in short, the endless ocean stretching and deepening from the first canto of
Paradiso to the last.[139]

Together with the tercet in which it comes to a climax, the passage sums up the
entire Christian tradition, from the Gospels and apostolic writings to St Augustine,
from the Scholastics to the mystics, including the declarations of St Clare of Assisi
herself. One can hear traces of the habitual greeting of Jesus, 'peace be with you', one
of the Beatitudes, 'Blessed are the peacemakers: for they shall be called the children of
God', and his words to the disciples, 'Peace I leave with you, my peace I give unto
you', the song of the angels at the nativity, 'on earth peace, good will towards men',

and the roar of the crowd at the entrance to Jerusalem, '*peace in heaven* and glory in the highest'; St Paul's claim to the Romans, 'the kingdom of God is not meat and drink, but righteousness, *and peace, and joy in the Holy Ghost*'; the great hymns to charity in the First Letter to the Corinthians and John's first Epistle: 'love is of God; and every one that loveth is born of God, and knoweth God. He that loveth not knoweth not God, for God is love' — *Deus caritas est*.[140]

The entire course of Augustine's *Confessions* is mirrored here, opening as they do with the famous sentence, 'you made us for yourself and our heart is restless until it is quieted in you', and coming to a close with a passage which Dante cannot have overlooked in writing cantos I–III of *Paradiso*: 'In your gift we find peace: there we enjoy you. Our peace is our place ... *In the good will is our peace*. Every body with its weight aims towards the place which is its own ... Fire aims upwards, stone downwards ... Everything which is outside of order is unstable, once ordered it finds peace'. Echoes can also be heard of the final chapters of *De civitate Dei*, which describe the nature of the vision of God which the blessed will have after resurrection ('in that region is found the peace of God which, as the Apostle says, passes all understanding') and discuss the 'degrees' of honour and glory which they will enjoy without anyone lower envying those in a higher position, but where peace is also celebrated: from that of the body, spiralling upwards to the peace of the Heavenly City, of all things and of the order which has arranged every thing in its appointed place: 'the peace of the Heavenly City is a perfectly ordered and fully concordant fellowship in the enjoyment of God and in mutual enjoyment by union with God; the peace of all things is a tranquillity of order. Order is the classification (*disposition*) of things equal and unequal that assigns to each its proper position'.[141]

The writings of the mystics are also to be found here, from Bernard of Clairvaux to St Ivo's *Epistle to Severinus on Charity*, to Richard of St Victor.[142] And St Clare's own inspiration as founder of the Order to which Piccarda belonged seems to be present too. 'Set your mind in the mirror of eternity', Clare wrote to Agnes of Bohemia, 'set your soul in the splendour of glory, set your heart in the figure of divine substance and, through contemplation, transform your whole self in the image of his divinity, so that by savouring the hidden sweetness which God has reserved right from the start for those who love him, you can hear what his friends hear'; and 'blessed poverty, holy humility, and ineffable charity shine in this mirror'.[143]

Bonaventure and Thomas Aquinas, the great Scholastics who together with the mystics appear in the Heaven of the Sun and speak in cantos X–XIII of *Paradiso* are of course no strangers to this way of thinking. Bonaventure ends his *Breviloquium* with a chapter devoted to the glory of Paradise, maintaining that here 'servabitur gradus et distinctio secundum exigentiam meritorum' and that the blessed soul will be made consonant with God, able to see him clearly, to love him fully with will, to rest wholly within Him, in Him 'finding peace, light, and everlasting sufficiency'.[144] Aquinas devotes two great *quaestiones* of the *Summa Theologiae* to beatitude and peace, the third of the Prima Secundae and the twenty-ninth of the Secunda Secundae, returning to the problem of the 'mansiones' or degrees of beatitude in *quaestio* 93 of the Supplement. All Dante's terms recur in the treatment by Thomas: the object of will, he maintains, is the perfect and universal good, but only God can 'quiet' will. The 'perfecta quietatio intellectus et voluntatis' brings beatitude. The 'sequela caritatis' is 'gaudium', and the perfection of 'gaudium' is peace. As product of charity 'secundum ipsam rationem dilectionis Dei', peace lies 'in quietatione et unione appetitus', and 'perfect' peace in the 'perfect fruition of the supreme Good', 'per quam omnes appetitus uniuntur quietati in uno'. As claimed in the First Epistle of John and in St Augustine, there are also 'mansiones' or varying degrees of beatitude: 'the more one is united with God, the more blessed one will be'. 'Sed secundum modum caritatis est modum coniunctionis ad Deum. Ergo secundum differentiam caritatis erit et diversitas beatitudinis'. In his commentary on the *De divinis nominibus* of Pseudo-Dionysius, Thomas also repeats these concepts, in particular in the *lectiones* devoted to peace. With reference precisely to Augustine's *De civitate Dei*, he there declares that the 'unity of peace' consists in the 'tranquillitas ordinis', for which first of all distinction and difference are required.[145]

In short, Dante draws upon a solid and coherent tradition and puts in Piccarda's mouth a hymn to charity and peace on a par with those of Paul, John, Dionysius, and Augustine. But what confers upon his *terzine* their distinctive trait is their organization into apparently logical argumentation and the perfectly circular nature of the proclamation.[146] The logical argument consists of five propositions which are consequentially linked: (i) the virtue of charity 'quiets' our will and makes us want only what we have; (ii) *if* we wished to be higher, our desires would discord with the will of God, who appoints the blessed to the various heavens; (iii) which is impossible in paradise, *since* it is necessary to be in charity there, and *if* the nature of charity is borne in mind; (iv) *therefore*, the division 'from height to height' 'is pleasing' to the whole of Paradise and to God, who 'invoglia', 'in-wills', the blessed to His will, making them desire what he wants; (v) hence, in his will lies our peace: that sea towards which all things move, both those created by him and those generated by nature.

This logic, however, is set out in two perfectly corresponding circles, forming an immense paradox and grand mystical tautology. The two principles by which it is inspired are those of God's will and charity. The first circle starts from the will of the blessed: dictated by charity, their will is fulfilled in their desiring only what they have. Thus, their distribution corresponds to the 'divina voglia', in which their 'voglie' become one. The second circle starts from their distribution: this distribution 'is pleasing' to the whole of Heaven and to God, who in his desire 'invoglia', informs and shapes the will of the blessed. In the will of God lies peace (as charity 'quiets' will). It is clear that these two circles have, as it were, divine will as their centre (the term 'will' is repeated four times), and the will of the blessed (repeated four times, and once as 'nostri disiri') as their radius. The circumference would then be the distribution of the blessed (twice) and above all the unity of their wills and the unity of their wills with God's ('tenersi dentro a la divina voglia, perch'una fansi nostre voglie stesse'; 'e 'n la sua volontade è nostra pace').

The 'paradoxical' and 'tautological' circularity of the *terzine* is what makes them seem such profound descriptions of truth and so aesthetically satisfying. T. S. Eliot, who uses these lines more than once in his own poetry, says that 'it is the mystery of the inequality, in blessedness, of the blessed. It is *all the same, and yet* each degree *differs*'.[147] In short, we are dealing with being's conforming to being (in transcendental terms, to Being), in which the joy (the 'beatitude') which is 'peace' is found: acceptance of the variety and diversity of being within love (within charity). A poet of our own days, Derek Walcott, calls it 'the Bounty': in his view, Dante's '*concentric radiance*', John Clare's 'bliss', and the extraordinary riches of Caribbean nature coincide here, so much so that 'the souls and sails of *circling* gulls rhyme with: || "*In sua volontate è nostra pace*," | In His will is our peace. Peace in white harbours, | in marinas whose masts agree, in crescent melons …'.[148]

*   *   *

Peace and quiet are alien to the *Streben* required by the post-Romantic sentiment of beauty. But it is not impossible even for us to feel what John Took has called *L'etterno piacer*.[149] The aesthetic dimension is prominent in *Paradiso* III from the moment Dante reminds us that Beatrice has, with her speech on the Heavens, revealed to him 'di bella verità … il dolce aspetto'. And Piccarda, whose brother Forese recalls in Purgatory her goodness and beauty, appears 'più bella' in Paradise, transformed as she is 'from former knowledge', because in her and the others' 'mirabili aspetti' 'risplende non so che divino' ['there shines forth I know not what of divine']. All the spirits (as Beatrice says in canto IV) 'fanno bello il primo giro', the Empyrean itself, where they have 'dolce vita' according to how intensely they experience 'the eternal breath'.[150]

The beauty which Paradise displays, and which Dante speaks of in the *Paradiso*, leads to knowledge and is one with truth, goodness, and peace. Here, the truth is God's truth 'in which every intellect finds rest':[151] just as in His will resides the 'peace' of the blessed, so He is the '*verace* luce che li *appaga*'.[152] The circles multiply. 'Eodem appetitu', writes Thomas Aquinas in the *De veritate*, 'appetitur bonum, pulchrum et pax'. Moreover, beauty adds to good an 'order' which pertains to knowledge, because sight — among all the senses the one giving most aesthetic pleasure — is a predominantly 'knowing' sense. Beauty, says Thomas, concerns the 'vis cognoscitiva'.[153] And it is for this reason that Dante can speak of the 'sweet aspect' of 'fair truth' and reply with enthusiasm to Beatrice's explanations in canto IV:

> Io veggio ben che già mai non si sazia
> nostro intelletto, se 'l ver non lo illustra
> di fuor dal qual nessun vero si spazia.

> [Well do I see that our intellect is never satisfied
> unless that truth enlighten it
> beyond which no truth can range.]

The 'etterno piacer' appears, in *Paradiso* III, 52–54, as the 'piacer', the 'pleasure of the Holy Ghost', as 'letizia' and *dulcedo*. But images of desire for food and satiety constitute, in all three cantos IV–V, 'sensible' correlatives of the process of knowledge.[154] The three medieval, and Thomist, criteria for beauty are inherent in the external appearance of the souls and the very nature of their blessedness: *claritas* with which the shades appear; *consonantia* of their distribution and degree; *integritas* as a 'forma totius, quae ex integritate partium consurgit' [form of the whole which rises from the integrity of the parts].[155] 'It is pleasing to the *whole* kingdom', and 'to which *all* things move', Piccarda already says in her speech: much later, however, at the end of his journey, Dante himself will contemplate 'la *forma* universal di questo nodo'.[156]

In the 'wondrous aspects' of the spirits of the first Heaven 'there shines forth I know not what of divine', a mere 'shadowy preface' of absolute Beauty. But after listening to Piccarda and Beatrice, Dante's mind also shines with this same light and truth, in an increasingly intense *claritas* as he rises through the spheres of Paradise. Beatrice notes this at the opening of canto V:

> Io veggio ben sì come già resplende
> ne l'intelletto tuo l'etterna luce,
> che, vista, sola e sempre amore accende.

> [Well do I see how there now shines
> in your mind the eternal light
> which, seen, alone and always kindles love.]

This is what Dante, in *Paradiso* XXVII, terms 'mente innamorata', the 'mind in love' which characterizes all of his philo-sophy, his love of wisdom: what he calls his 'cupido ingegno', the 'eager mind'.[157] The meeting with Piccarda is a key moment in this love story: indeed, the explanations in cantos IV and V derive from it. They are central in themselves, and linked to each other both by the semantic domain of will-vow[158] and in a process of knowledge whose nature the pilgrim reveals to Beatrice with passionate fervour. This process starts from the truth which is God, which alone can placate human desire for knowledge and outside of which there can be no truth, and returns — once more in a sweeping circle — to the 'sommo', the summit. Human intellect is quieted in that truth as soon as it reaches it, just as wild animals rest in their dens: and — a claim of rare intellectual strength and faith — it *can* reach this truth, otherwise every desire for knowledge, natural in human beings, would be in vain. But just as a new shoot grows at the root of a plant, so from that desire springs, 'at the foot of truth', doubt, and this too is a natural impulse, urging us from one height to the next, towards the summit of supreme truth:

> Io veggio ben che già mai non si sazia
> nostro intelletto, se 'l ver non lo illustra
> di fuor dal qual nessun vero si spazia.
>   Posasi in esso, come fera in lustra,
> tosto che giunto l'ha; e giugner puollo:
> se non, ciascun disio sarebbe *frustra*.
>   Nasce per quello, a guisa di rampollo,
> a piè del vero il dubbio; ed è natura
> ch'al sommo pinge noi di collo in collo.[159]

> [Well do I see that our intellect is never satisfied
> unless that truth enlighten it
> beyond which no truth can range.
> In that it rests, like a beast in its lair,
> as soon as it gains it; and gain it it can,
> else every desire would be vain.
> Because of this, doubt springs up like a shoot,
> at the foot of truth; and it is nature
> that urges us to the summit, from height to height.]

Complementing the *terzina* in *Purgatorio* XXI which precedes Statius' appearance, these lines emphasize the natural and gradual passage from truth to truth[160] as earlier in her speech Piccarda had underlined the essentiality ('è formale') of the blessed state and the distribution by degrees of the souls in Paradise. The desire for knowledge, predicated at the start of Aristotle's *Metaphysics* and Dante's *Convivio*, is here seen as akin to animal appetite, that of wild beasts, and its object, truth, as the prey towards which that appetite is directed.[161] At the same time, the doubt which unites with desire in urging towards the search is imagined as the shoot of a plant, as though in speaking of man's highest goal Dante wanted to recall the *instinct* towards truth, parallel to that 'istinto' which, according to *Paradiso* I, leads each creature to its 'port' in the great sea of being. It is as though through metaphor he wanted to echo another truth: the three stages — vegetable, animal, and rational — of man's generation-creation described by Statius in canto xxv of *Purgatorio*.

Most certainly a mind in love: enamoured of its own goal, and of the process leading it there, representing in a nutshell the progress through the whole of *Paradiso*: 'al sommo' 'di collo in collo'. And a mind enamoured of its own doubts, which are an organic part of that process. This is intellectual *pulchritudo*, in which the 'etterno piacer' is shown as pleasure in learning. Mind in love and peace are the two poles of beauty in cantos III and IV of *Paradiso*: one, so to speak, *in via*, and the other *in fine* — *in porto*.

* * *

From the encounter with Piccarda, as if they were shoots of a plant, spring the questions of the following cantos, dealing with the four problems of the localization of souls in Heaven, the Scriptures' way of speaking, absolute and relative will, and the possibility of compensating for a neglected vow or obtaining a dispensation from it. These questions may seem less than thrilling to us, but to a writer such as Dante they are of primary importance, since they touch on the very essence of the Kingdom of Heaven, the way to describe it, human will between the choice of martyrdom and acceptance of a lesser evil, the freedom of man and his pact with God: and thus, in short, the metaphysical-theological, as well as the ethical and poetic dimensions.

I shall leave aside the first two domains,[162] but I would like to say a few words about the third, for it is here that the specific *pulchritudo* of the *Paradiso* takes shape. Beatrice explains to Dante that the souls of the blessed do *not* return to Heaven, as Plato seems to say in the *Timaeus*, and that the shades of Piccarda and Constance do not dwell in the Heaven of the Moon but simply appear there: they are actually in the Empyrean like the 'Seraphim that is most made one with God', or Moses, Samuel, John the Baptist, John the Evangelist, and Mary. Beatrice in fact maintains that these souls *show themselves* in this sphere 'per far segno' ['in sign'] of their condition as spirits.[163] She adds:

> Così parlar conviensi al vostro ingegno,
> però che solo da sensato apprende
> ciò che fa poscia d'intelletto degno.
>   Per questo la Scrittura condescende
> a vostra facultate, e piedi e mano
> attribuisce a Dio e altro intende;
>   e Santa Chiesa con aspetto umano
> Gabrïel e Michel vi rappresenta,
> e l'altro che Tobia rifece sano.[164]

> [It is necessary to speak thus to your faculty,
> since only from sense perception does it grasp

that which it then makes fit for the intellect.
For this reason Scripture condescends
to your capacity and attributes hands
and feet to God, having another meaning,
and Holy Church represents to you with human
aspect Gabriel and Michael
and the other who made Tobit whole again.]

These *terzine* clearly link Dante's *Paradiso* to the Scriptures and to Church practice: 'to speak *thus*' refers directly to the description in canto III, where the souls appear 'per far segno', while the two following *terzine*, explicitly tied to the first ('per questo') concern the Bible and the images, particularly those of angels, used in churches both as visual representations and as examples in preaching. They are first of all a declaration of cultural belonging: to the long ecclesiastical tradition which justifies icons;[165] to the civilization of representation of the divine which underwent a new and extraordinary artistic blossoming in Italy between the thirteenth and fourteenth centuries. They are also, however, the distillation of 'symbolic' theories which continue from Pseudo-Dionysius up to the great Scholastics.[166] In his treatise on divine names, the Areopagite had in fact claimed that, inspired by the 'divine apparitions which take place in sacred temples or elsewhere', the theologians gave to the supreme Good names reflecting 'his causal functions and powers' and attributed to him 'human shapes and figures', or the forms of fire or amber. 'Thus they praise', he continued, promising to deal with the topic more fully in the *Symbolic Theology*, 'his eyes and ears, his hair, face, hands and shoulders, wings, arms, back, feet'.[167] Thomas Aquinas, who comments on this passage in his *Expositio* on *De divinis nominibus*, sums up and extends the meditation in his *Summa Theologiae*. 'It is fitting (*conveniens est*: Dante's 'conviensi') for the Holy Scriptures to deal with divine and spiritual things under the likeness of bodily things', he claims, because God provides for all creatures according to their nature and it is natural for man to arrive at things of the intellect through those of the senses 'for all knowledge begins with the senses' ('quia omnis nostra cognitio a sensu initium habet'; in Dante our 'ingegno … solo da sensato apprende'). Thus, 'it is fitting' that in the Scriptures spiritual things are transmitted to us 'under the metaphor of bodily things' and 'in a common manner', so that the ignorant (the *rudes*) may also understand them. Moreover, the light of divine revelation is not destroyed by the 'sensible figures by which it is hidden', but 'remains within its truth, in such a way as to prevent the minds to which it appears from stopping at semblances, but rather elevate them to the knowledge of intelligible things'. And finally, 'as Dionysius says', 'it is fitting that the divine things be transmitted, in the Scriptures, in the shape of vile bodies rather than noble ones': in part because the human mind can thus free itself first of the error into which it would fall by thinking that it is possible to represent the divine by means of noble bodies, and in part because this way is more fit to the knowledge which we have of God in this life, in part because divine things are thus more easily hidden from those unworthy of them. When Scripture 'names the arm of God', it does not do so in a literal and corporeal sense, but indicates his 'operative virtue'.[168]

Dante seems to accept these indications only in part. In claiming that the Bible gives God human limbs 'e altro intende', and in adding that Plato's 'sentenza', when he says that the soul returns 'to its star', is also perhaps 'd'altra guisa | che la voce non suona',

Dante is echoing typical medieval definitions of allegory.[169] But he is generally careful not to use such anthropomorphic images of the divine, perhaps because the 'nostra effige' 'painted' in God's own essence — the Incarnation — concentrates and sums up in perfect Christian fashion all the human representation and truth that He can bear.[170] On the contrary, he uses metaphors derived from philosophical and theological discourse: love, shining, substance, point, potency, act. In short he seems to choose the way of speaking of God which Dionysius and Thomas Aquinas call 'per intelligibiles processiones'.[171] When he opts for 'sensibiles similitudines', he uses not 'vile' things, but those which are 'noble': light, ray, fire, sea.

If he is using allegory, this is once or twice removed from the experience of the 'rudes'. When he speaks of the divine in *Paradiso*, Dante none the less uses 'sensible' 'metaphors' and 'figures', but elevates them to the lofty and rarefied register of his own lyric poetry.[172] As the poet of plurilingualism and of the 'sermo humilis', he often chooses his icons among 'corporeal' things, but immerses them in *claritas*, enveloping them with neoplatonic brightness, alternating them with discourses dominated by mystical circularity, referring to the precise terminology of Aristotelian and Scholastic thought. His is, in short, totally 'intellectual' allegory. While always attentive to detail, he sees it, so to speak, *sub specie integritatis*, as an element of universal order, within the perfection of the whole. He attends to degrees, to the 'più e meno', while safeguarding the *consonantia*, the due proportion of each thing to another.

He thus establishes a relationship not between things and words, but between two different languages. If there is a hiatus between letter and allegory, it depends on that relationship:[173] on the evocative void between one sphere and the next, between our understanding and our misunderstanding of 'love' or 'splendour'. The same hiatus saves the dramatic-theological fiction of the *cantica*: the spirits of the First Heaven appear in the Moon, but only 'per far segno' of their 'spiritual' lot, of their actual celestial state, which consists of their being distributed in the Empyrean according to degree. Here, Dante gives a special twist to the 'allegory of theologians' which is at one and the same time theological and poetic, just as he had done by speaking of shades and inventing for them a physiology and a metaphysics. In this sense, the correspondence between the theory expounded by Statius in *Purgatorio* XXV and springing from the pilgrim's doubts after meeting with Forese, and that illustrated by Beatrice and stemming from the doubts arising after the episode with Piccarda.

In *Paradiso* III, the metaphorical language is a 'shadowy preface' of the splendour which it will gradually acquire in the *cantica*.[174] The spirits of the First Heaven still appear as shades, and the similes depicting their appearance rest upon transparent and still glass, on limpid and tranquil waters, on the pearl which shines upon a white forehead. The souls of the Second Heaven will also appear as shades, and the simile describing their appearance returns, in canto V, to water 'tranquilla e pura', now that of a fishpond. But the shades have become 'splendori', and each of them is seen 'by the bright effulgence' that comes forth from it. The one which will be identified as Justinian 'nests in his own light', and its smiling eyes sparkle. For this shade Dante then draws a comparison with the sun which hides on account of an excess of light when its heat has consumed the vapours tempering its splendour: in the same way the 'holy figure' of Justinian hides 'within its own rays'. Piccarda was a shade surrounded by *claritas*, mere brightness. Justinian is a shade surrounded by blinding light. This is clearly a development.

At the start of canto III, Beatrice urges Dante to speak with the spirits of the First Heaven, to listen to them and believe them. When the souls of the Heaven of Mercury appear in canto v, she repeats: 'Dì, dì | sicuramente, e credi' ['Speak, speak with confidence, and believe them']. The formula is the same: what changes is that in the first case the request for Dante to have faith is based on the fact that the spirits are linked to God by the light of his truth, which satisfies them and 'da sé non lascia lor torcer li piedi' ['does not let them turn their steps aside from it'], to the point that in their appearance shines forth *'non so che* divino' ['something divine'], while in the second the blessed are themselves 'come dii' [like gods].[175] Thus, in the developing *deificatio* which takes place in Paradise, and which includes the angelic orders up to the Seraphim, 'che più s'india' ['which is most in God'],[176] the spirits of the Heaven of the Moon occupy the first stage. Corresponding to this is the first level of the *pulchritudo* which derives from union with God and from the display of his grace and goodness: 'non mi ti celerà l'esser più bella' ['my being more beautiful will not conceal me from you'].

✻   ✻   ✻

That Dante has chosen precisely a Donati woman to represent this incipient theme of beauty can hardly be a matter of chance. The leitmotif of metamorphosis, and the echoes of Ovid, link the members of the Donati family, spread as they are across Hell, Purgatory, and Paradise.[177] But this theme is closely tied to the other, that of *form*. The shape of the thieves and falsifiers, including Cianfa and Buoso, is distorted, confused, unnatural, capable of changing 'materia', disintegrated, lost.[178] The shape of the penitent gluttons, including Forese is 'cangiata', made lean, hollowed, spectral. The shape of the women who did not fulfil their vows, including Piccarda is transmuted, made more beautiful. And 'form', for Dante as for Aristotle, means the necessary essence, the substance of things which have matter: the thing's cause or *raison d'être*, that which makes it what it is; the act or actuality of the thing itself; the beginning and aim of its becoming. For Dante, to speak of form means to go straight to the heart of things and people. This is why the theme of recognition is so important in these cantos.

The Donati family's journey from *Inferno* to *Paradiso* marks the passage not only from fraudulent theft to penitent gluttony and to charity — and therefore from deceit to greed and to love — but also from *turpe* to *pulchrum*, from the perverse, inhuman, snakelike, and paradiabolical image of the thieves, to the sublime, more than human, pre-divine image of the spirits in the Heaven of the Moon. In between, we encounter the image, so profoundly human — of skin which 'cleaves' to the bones — of the gluttons in Purgatory. The icon of man under the letters O, M, and O: and of 'omo' at the extreme end of his own experience, at the passage from death to 'better life'. An image in transition, suspended between cannibal and executioner, between Erisychthon and Mary of Eleazarus (almost an Ugolino, so to speak), on the one hand, and sacrificial victim, Jesus calling out from the cross, on the other.

In each of these figures, the original form — the 'primaio aspetto' of *Inferno* XXV, the 'ciò che l'aspetto in sé avea conquiso' of *Purgatorio* XXIII, the 'primi concetti' of *Paradiso* III — has disappeared: the earthly, historical identity of the people as they were in life has gone. This is certainly a useful lesson on the effects of dying and on the nature of the shades in the afterlife. But the transformation also has various outcomes. There are plenty of twisted limbs, and of 'matter' sprouting forth and being drawn in again, among the thieves: wasting away and 'lack of flesh', among the gluttons: evanescent *claritas*, among the blessed of the first Heaven. In short, we witness a gradual loss of corporeality, an increasingly intense acquisition of spirituality.[179]

Yet, as far as ties to history are concerned, it seems quite the opposite. The Donati are connected to Dante by a complex web of economic, political, and kinship relations. These seem to be reflected in the poem with strength inversely proportional to reality. Dante says absolutely nothing about the earthly life of Cianfa and Buoso Donati. He reveals little more about Forese, and all on the level of the individual person: gluttony, a praying wife, a friend lost and found. When it comes to Piccarda, however, he tells of her flight from the world and the world's violence to her. In the text, Piccarda lives and suffers within history. History seems to have had greater impact on her than on her relatives in Hell and Purgatory. It is as though Piccarda had atoned for history by living.

She has borne and still bears the burden of the actions ('uomini poi ...') of Corso, the brother whom Forese evokes by dashing him from his steed straight into Hell. Corso is the nightmare of history, and within the trinity of the Donati siblings he represents damnation. Piccarda has suffered on account of that nightmare: by expiating she has paid history's ransom. Located at the centre of that trinity — because it is he who speaks of his brother and sister — Forese seems to have lived outside history. His existence appears to be an entirely personal story of excess: in eating and drinking, in composing 'poesia giocosa'. The meeting with his friend is necessary for Forese to return — now that he is in Purgatory — to history: to Corso, to the Florentine women. Dante chooses precisely the conversation with Forese, at the centre of the sequence, to juxtapose history and metahistory: his journey in the afterlife, from Virgil to Beatrice, from the deep night 'de' veri morti' to the Mount of Purgatory and to Paradise. The meeting with the Donati has meant writing a *Commedia* within the *Commedia*.

The image of the poem thus dramatically dominates the discourse on poetry with which the meetings with Forese, Bonagiunta, and Statius (and later with Guinizzelli and Arnaut) deal in equally dramatic terms. But poetry is also an essential topic of the cantos I have looked at, which in fact outline a series of poetics: of metamorphosis, of the shade, of universal order; of the uncanny, of waiting, of *pulchritudo*. Dante is careful to draw our attention to this constantly: proclaiming his 'vanto' over Ovid and Lucan, declaring his own 'novità', apologizing for his pen which 'abborra'; indicating love and Love as his primary source; pointing out the *dulcedo* of his poetry and of the *Paradiso*; explaining the very mechanisms of his own poetic-theological fiction: the nature of the shade, the appearance of the spirits in the First Heaven 'per far segno' of their true lot.

There is one word which links the beginning and end of what at this point I would call the 'poetics of the Donati': *smagare*. At the centre of the sequence it is replaced by the wonder and desire for knowledge that Dante shows when he meets Forese.[180] But in the case of the thieves and of Piccarda, it is *smagare* that dominates: bewilderment, being overwhelmed. There is, however, an important point to remember: the 'animo smagato' of *Inferno* xxv is a *consequence* of the spectacle that Dante has witnessed in the seventh *bolgia*; the 'smaga' of *Paradiso* III *precedes* the conversation with Piccarda. In the second instance, Dante describes himself as overcome by the excess of desire he experiences in wishing to speak to the shade who herself seems 'più vaga di ragionar'. This bewildered desire is a reciprocal desire to communicate. The first time, it was confusion and afterwards *dismay*. Here, it is love and communion. In Hell, it was an overwhelming sense of irredeemable loss: in Paradise, it is the bewilderment of an overly-intense thirst, of a mind in love with truth, peace, and beauty. We are moving closer now to the white rose where Rachel sits without ever deflecting her gaze from the mirror of her own mind, of contemplation. Rachel 'mai non si smaga / dal suo miraglio'.[181]

NOTES

* Quotations from the *Divina Commedia* are taken from *La Commedia secondo l'antica vulgata*, ed. by G. Petrocchi (Florence: Le Lettere, 1994²), and the accompanying English translations, with occasional modifications, from *The Divine Comedy of Dante Alighieri*, trans. and comm. by J. D. Sinclair, 3 vols (London: John Lane The Bodley Head, 1939–46). The Bible is quoted in English in the Authorized Version; Latin classics, in sometimes modified form, from the Loeb Classics series. Other English translations are entirely my own.

[1] For the Donati family see R. Piattoli, entry on 'Donati', in *Enciclopedia Dantesca*, 6 vols (Rome: Istituto dell'Enciclopedia Italiana, 1970–78), II (1970), 555–57; R. Davidsohn, *Storia di Firenze* (Florence: Sansoni, 1956–68), *ad indicem*; C. Lansing, *The Florentine Magnates: Lineage and Faction in a Medieval Commune* (Princeton: Princeton University Press, 1991).

[2] The sources of the story are the Pseudo-Brunetto chronicles (*Cronica pseudolatiniana*, in appendix to P. Villari, *I primi due secoli della storia di Firenze*, II (Florence: Sansoni, 1893), 233–34), Villani (G. Villani, *Nuova cronica*, ed. by G. Porta (Parma, Guanda–Fondazione Bembo, 1990); *Istorie fiorentine* (Milan: Soc. Tip. Classici Italiani, 1802–03)), and Compagni (who erroneously names Oderigo Giantruffetti as father of Buondelmonte's betrothed). The sentences quoted are from Dino Compagni, *Cronica*, ed. by G. Luzzatto (Turin: Einaudi, 1968), I ii, 7–9. For the lines from Dante see *Inferno* XXVIII, 106–08, and *Paradiso* XVI, 136–47.

[3] See the entries by E. Ragni, 'Donati, Cianfa' and R. Piattoli, 'Donati, Buoso', in *Enciclopedia Dantesca*, II, 558 and 557–58; R. Piattoli, 'Buoso', ibid., I (1970), 726–27; and M. Barbi, 'A proposito di Buoso Donati ricordato nel canto XXX dell'*Inferno*', now in his *Problemi di critica dantesca*, 1st series (Florence: Sansoni, 1975), pp. 305–22.

[4] Dante Alighieri, *Rime*, ed. by Domenico De Robertis, 3 vols in 5 (Florence: Le Lettere, 2002), III, 459.

[5] My account of these events follows Compagni, *Cronica*, I xx–xxii.

[6] Ibid., I xxi, 48–49.

[7] Ibid., II xx, 98.

[8] *Inferno* VI, 64–75.

[9] Davidsohn, *Storia*, III and IV, passim; I. Del Lungo, *I Bianchi e i Neri* (Milan: Hoepli, 1921); E. Sestan, 'Donati, Corso', in *Enciclopedia Dantesca*, II, 558–60.

[10] *Purgatorio* XXIV, 79–82.

[11] Compagni, *Cronica*, III xxi; Villani, IX xcvi.

[12] *Benvenuti de Rambaldis de Imola comentum super Dantis Aldigherij Comoediam*, ed. by I. P. Lacaita (Florence: Barbèra, 1887) *ad Purgatorio* XXIV, 82–84.

[13] The 'crescendo sempre' ('still gaining speed') of line 86 doubtless refers to speed, but also outlines for readers the increasingly gigantic shadow of the beast.

[14] *Purgatorio* XXIV, 94–97.

[15] This is the direct descendent of the 'ignitos serpentes' with which the Vulgate translates the Hebrew *saraf* of Numbers 21. 6: see V. Russo, *La pena dei ladri*, in *Sussidi di esegesi dantesca* (Naples: Liguori, 1966), pp. 129–46 (p. 141). The episode of the snakes in Numbers is interpreted as the 'umbra' of Christ's death by John Scotus Eriugena, *Commentarius in Evangelium secundum Joannem*, *Patrologia Latina* CXXII, 320 A–C.

[16] The association between serpents and pepper dates back at least to the *Liber monstrorum de diversis generibus*, III, 6. See C. Bologna's edition (Milan: Bompiani, 1977), pp. 142–43, in which it is said that 'where Arabia merges with the Red Sea certain serpents are to be found, and with them white pepper. Men set the place alight, and when the serpents flee underground they gather the pepper, now blackened by the flames licking it'.

[17] *Epistole* VII, 7, 23–26.

[18] As Thomas explicitly recalls in *Summa Theologiae* II–II, q. 66, a. 2, resp. For the 'social' aspect of theft, see D. Mattalia, 'Canto XXV', in *Lectura Dantis Scaligera. Inferno* (Florence: Le Monnier, 1967), pp. 891–929 (p. 928).

[19] *Monarchia* I xi 11, with reference to *Nicomachean Ethics* V, 2, 1129 a32–b 10; *Inferno* VII, 70–96: see R. Kirkpatrick, '*Inferno* XXV', in *Cambridge Readings in Dante's Comedy*, ed. by K. Foster and P. Boyde (Cambridge: Cambridge University Press, 1981), pp. 23–48 (pp. 24–25), developed further in R. Kirkpatrick, *Dante's Inferno: Difficulty and Dead Poetry* (Cambridge: Cambridge University Press, 1987), pp. 310–24.

[20] Genesis 1. 26; the citation is from Thomas, *Summa Theologiae* II–II, q. 66, a. 1, resp.

[21] Russo, *La pena dei ladri*, p. 138.

[22] *Liber Sententiarum* II, XVI, 4, 2.

[23] Genesis 3. 1 and 14; Revelation 20. 2; Augustine, *De Genesi contra Manichaeos* II, XIV, 20; and see *De Genesi ad litteram* XI, II–IV, 4–6.

[24] It should be noted that in presenting the thieves naked and bound by serpents Dante is going against the legend, widespread in the Middle Ages and confirmed by the *Physiologus* (13), according to which serpents attack a clothed man but flee upon seeing one naked. The snake did not succeed in attacking Adam, explains the *Physiologus*, since he was naked, but as soon as he dressed in a tunic ('that is, the mortality of the carnal and sinning body'), it attacked him: see *Physiologus*, trans. by M. J. Curley (Austin–London: University of Texas Press, 1979), pp. 16–19; *Physiologus*, ed. by F. Sbordone (facs. Hildesheim: Olms, 1991, of Rome: Dante Alighieri–Albrighi, Segati, 1936), pp. 36–44. See also Isidore, *Etymologiae* XII, iv, 48.

[25] *Inferno* XXV, 14 and 18; *Paradiso* XIX, 46 and 48. Vanni is also the subject of a terrifying re-Creation (from the 'dust of the ground', Genesis 2. 6) in lines 103–05 of canto XXIV, where, first reduced to ashes and fallen to the ground, the dust gathers 'together of itself', and takes on its human shape: see R. Hollander, 'Ad ira parea mosso': God's voice in the Garden (*Inferno* XXIV, 69)', *Dante Studies*, 101 (1983), 27–49; Idem, 'Dante's georgic (*Inferno* XXIV, 1–21)', ibid., 102 (1984), 111–21.

[26] See Russo, *La pena dei ladri*, pp. 139–41, with quotations also from Tommaseo's commentary.

[27] *Inferno* XXV, 4–9; *Aeneid* II, 201–27.

[28] But he separates him explicitly (XXV, 28–30) from his brother centaurs, placed in charge of the 'mere' violent in *Inferno* XII, 55–99. The dragon is for Isidore (*Etymologiae* XII, iv, 4) 'the largest of all the *serpents*': with which Dante completely covers Cacus.

[29] See E. Paratore, *Tradizione e struttura in Dante* (Florence: Sansoni, 1968), pp. 250–80 (pp. 254–60).

[30] See G. K. Galinsky, 'The Hercules–Cacus Episode in *Aeneid* VIII', *American Journal of Philology*, 87 (1966), 18–51; id., *The Herakles Theme* (Oxford: Blackwell, 1972), pp. 131–49; M. Simon, *Hercule et le Christianisme* (Strasbourg–Paris: Les Belles Lettres, 1955); E. Panofsky, *Studies in Iconology* (New York: Harper, 1962), p. 19.

[31] *Epistole* VII (as cited also for the viper and the smoke), 2, 10 and 7, 20. See R. Kirkpatrick, '*Inferno* XXV', p. 30.

[32] *Inferno* XXV, 58–59: *Metamorphoses* IV, 365; *Inferno* XXV, 70–72: *Metamorphoses* IV, 378–79; *Inferno* XXV, 61–62: *Pharsalia* IX, 781–82.

[33] *Inferno* XXV, 94–99: *Pharsalia* IX, 761–804; *Metamorphoses* IV, 563–603.

[34] See G. Almansi, *L'estetica dell'osceno* (Turin: Einaudi, 1974), pp. 39–88.

[35] With Hugh of Saint Victor: see E. De Bruyne, *Études d'esthétique médiévale*, 2 vols (now Paris: Albin Michel, 1998), I, 585–86.

[36] With Bonaventure: see De Bruyne, *Études*, II, 221–22.

[37] See Kirkpatrick, '*Inferno* XXV', pp. 41–42; L. Barkan, *The Gods Made Flesh: Metamorphosis and the Pursuit of Paganism* (New Haven: Yale University Press, 1986), pp. 137–70.

[38] *Commedia*, ed. by E. Pasquini and A. Quaglio (Milan: Garzanti, 1987), ad *Inferno* XXV, 85–86.

[39] Also of the creation of the individual soul by God and the formation of the shadow which survives beyond death: *Purgatorio* XXV, 67–108.

[40] See Kirkpatrick, 'Inferno xxv', p. 25; Hollander, 'Dante's georgic', pp. 111–21. See also important discussions by A. Oldcorn, 'Canto xxv. The perverse image', in *Lectura Dantis. Inferno*, ed. by A. Mandelbaum, A. Oldcorn and C. Ross (Berkeley–Los Angeles–London: University of California Press, 1998), pp. 328–47; and R. L. Martinez, 'Time and the thief', in R. M. Durling and R. L. Martinez, *Inferno* (New York–Oxford: Oxford University Press, 1996), pp. 568–71.

[41] *Inferno* xxv, 100–11; *Metamorphoses* xv, 392–400.

[42] See Paratore, *Tradizione e struttura*, pp. 273–74.

[43] To be precise, as follows: one-another (42), one (51), one-another (63), two (67), two-one (69), two-one (70), two-one-two: zero (71–72), two-zero (77), two-one-one (83–86), one-other (92), two-two (100–01), one-other (118), one-other (121), one-other (136–38); without counting the serpent's six feet and their subdivision, the 'one check and the other' (54), both thighs (55–56), the two arms made of the four lengths (73), 'the brute's two paws' (113), the two-one-two (feet-penis-penises, 115–17), the 'one hand' and 'the other' (120); and see Paratore, p. 274.

[44] *Inferno* xxv, 64–66: *Paradiso* xiv, 40–57.

[45] *Paradiso* xxxiii, 112–14; see Kirkpatrick, 'Inferno xxv', p. 46.

[46] See Martinez, 'Time and the thief', pp. 570–71.

[47] *Divina Commedia* con il commento di A. M. Chiavacci Leonardi, 3 vols (Milan: Mondadori, 1991), *ad Inferno* xxv, 101. See also D. De Robertis, 'Lo scempio delle umane proprietadi (*Inf.* xxiv e xxv)', *Bullettino storico pistoiese*, 14 (1979), 37–60.

[48] See also what Calcidius says in his commentary on *Timaeus* 309, ed. by C. Moreschini (Milan: Bompiani, 2003), pp. 616–17: 'the transformation takes place within matter, but not in the sense that matter itself undergoes change; rather, it concerns the qualities found and contained within matter. For if matter itself changes, it must transform into something else and cease to be matter: but this is surely absurd. In fact, as when *wax* is moulded into many different *shapes*, it is not the wax itself that changes, but its *figures*, while the wax remains unto its *nature* — since the shapes are not the wax itself …'.

[49] *Liber Sententiarum* ii, xvi, 3, 20–21.

[50] *Inferno* xvii, 110: Icarus has of course, since Ovid, been an example of the overturning of natural laws. See also *Convivio* ii, ix, 7: 'se la cera avesse spirito da temere, più temerebbe di venire a lo raggio del sole che non farebbe la pietra, però che la sua disposizione riceve quello per più forte operazione'; the image is taken from Aristotle, *De anima* iii, 12, 435a 2–3.

[51] *Purgatorio* xxxiii, 79–80; for this whole aspect see P. Boyde, *Dante Philomythes and Philosopher. Man in the Cosmos* (Cambridge: Cambridge University Press, 1981), pp. 224–29; and his *Perception and Passion in Dante's Comedy* (Cambridge: Cambridge University Press, 1993), pp. 15–17.

[52] Aristotle, *Physics* i, 9, 192a 22, cit. Boyde, *Dante Philomythes*, p. 367, n. 68.

[53] Cf. E. Sanguineti, *Interpretazione di Malebolge* (Florence: Olschki, 1961), pp. 173–207.

[54] In Freud's specific meaning of the term in 'The Uncanny'. See *The Standard Edition of the Complete Psychological Works of Sigmund Freud*, trans. and ed. by J. Strachey, 24 vols (London: Hogarth Press, 1953–74), xvii (1955): *An Infantile Neurosis and Other Works*, pp. 238–42. See also Almansi, *Estetica*, pp. 45 and 78: Almansi considers *Inferno* xxiv 'uno dei modelli fondamentali del processo artistico: la trasformazione del familiare nel non-familiare' and sees *Inferno* xxv as an example of the 'processo opposto: la familiarizzazione del fantastico, la trasformazione dell'irrealtà atemporale in una storica quotidianità'. But this second process is *uncanny* precisely in the Freudian sense: 'the uncanny is that class of the frightening … which is familiar and long-established in the mind' ('The Uncanny', p. 241).

[55] Smoke and fever ('aguta') are linked again in *Inferno* xxx, 91–99.

[56] See also J. T. Chiampi, 'The fate of writing: the punishment of thieves in the *Inferno*', and R. J. Ellrich, 'Envy, identity, and creativity: *Inferno* xxiv–xxv', both in *Dante Studies*, 102 (1984), 51–60 and 61–80.

[57] Cf. C. A. Cioffi, 'The anxieties of Ovidian influence: theft in *Inferno* xxiv and xxv', *Dante Studies*, 112 (1994), 77–100.

[58] For which see W. Ginsberg, *Dante's Aesthetics of Being* (Ann Arbor: University of Michigan Press, 1999), pp. 115–59.

[59] *Purgatorio* III, 11; XXVII, 104; X, 106.

[60] Where transitive, 'to render powerless', 'to confuse', or 'to lead astray', or 'remove'; where reflexive, 'to lose strength', 'to become weaker'. The overall meaning is that of *smarrire*, *smarrimento*: see K. Foster and P. Boyde, *Dante's Lyric Poetry* (Oxford: Clarendon Press, 1967), II: *Commentary*, pp. 116–17. See *Vita Nuova* XII, 13, 4 (*Ballata, i' voi*, 28); *Donna pietosa*, 37; *Doglia mi reca*, 124; *Fiore* II, 1.

[61] *Purgatorio* XIX, 20; *Paradiso* III, 36. For all this, see also the entries 'dismagare' and 'smagare' in *Enciclopedia Dantesca*, II, 499–500, and V, 274; 'smagare' in *Grande dizionario della lingua italiana*, founded by S. Battaglia, directed by G. Bárberi Squarotti, 21 vols (Turin: UTET, 1961–2002), XIX (1998), 132–33; and the commentaries of D. De Robertis and G. Gorni on *Vita nuova* (Milan–Naples: Ricciardi, 1980), p. 80; (Turin: Einaudi, 1996), p. 62. 'Smagare' is akin to Old French 'esmaier' and Provençal 'esmagar', ultimately deriving from a root 'exmagare', clearly formed by adding the Latin prefix 'ex' to Germanic 'magan'. The English 'dismay' (from Old French 'desmayer') is the only current survival of the word.

[62] For both, see P. Boitani, *The Tragic and the Sublime in Medieval Literature* (Cambridge: Cambridge University Press, 1989), pp. 20–40 and 250–78.

[63] In *Inferno* the metamorphoses of the thieves, among whom we find Cianfa and Buoso Donati, take up the whole of canto XXV, while the counterfeiting of Buoso by Simone Donati and Gianni Schicchi is evoked in canto XXX; in *Purgatorio*, two entire cantos, XXIII and XXIV, are devoted to Forese, whose appearance gives rise to the question leading to Statius's explanation of the generation of man and the formation of shades in canto XXV; in *Paradiso*, the whole of canto III dwells on the meeting with Piccarda, which generates the questions and answers in cantos IV and V on the true seat of the blessed and on the will.

[64] On recognition see Boyde, *Perception and Passion*, pp. 105–12; and in general T. Cave, *Recognitions. A Study in Poetics* (Oxford: Clarendon Press, 1988); P. Boitani, *The Tragic and the Sublime*, pp. 115–79; *The Bible and its Rewritings* (Oxford: Oxford University Press, 1999), pp. 1–57 and 130–205; *The Genius to Improve an Invention* (Notre Dame–London: University of Notre Dame Press, 2002), pp. 1–45 and 89–138.

[65] I have discussed this in *The Tragic and the Sublime*, pp. 142–76.

[66] Genesis 2. 9.

[67] See E. Auerbach, *Mimesis* (Princeton: Princeton University Press, 1968), pp. 180–81.

[68] Psalms, 102. 5, 'By reason of the voice of my groaning my bones cleave to my skin'; Job, 19. 20, 'My bone cleaveth to my skin'; Lamentations, 4. 8, 'their skin cleaveth to their bones; it is withered, it is become like a stick': see M. Marti, *Studi su Dante* (Galatina: Congedo, 1984); and R. L. Martinez, 'Dante's Forese, the Book of Job, and the office of the dead: a note on *Purgatorio* 25', *Dante Studies*, 120 (2002), 1–16.

[69] Ovid, *Metamorphoses*, VIII, 739–878; for the siege on Jerusalem and Mary of Eleazarus the ultimate source is Flavius Josephus, *De bello judaico* VI, 3, 201–13; the story is told in Orosius, *Historiae* VII, 9; John of Salisbury, *Policraticus* II, 6; Vincent of Beauvais, *Speculum historiale* X, 5.

[70] See C. Lund Mead, '*Domine, labia mea aperies*': Forese Donati and Ugolino', *Quaderni d'italianistica*, 10 (1989), 315–21.

[71] For the close Brunetto–Forese parallels, and for other echoes in the *Commedia*, see R. M. Durling and R. L. Martinez, *Purgatorio* (Oxford: Oxford University Press, 2003), pp. 393, 398–99, and 612–14, and references therein.

[72] Recognition with Brunetto is rather different and more troubled, taking place as it does in physical darkness where no sign of light appears ('favilla', 'raccese').

[73] Proust, *A la recherche du temps perdu*, dir. J.-Y. Tadié, 4 vols (Paris: Gallimard, 1987–89), IV (1989), 523.

[74] *Convivio* III viii 7; and see Vasoli's commentary, *ad loc*.

[75] *Poetics* 11, 1452a 30–34.

[76] *Convivio* IV i 1 and IV xxv 1, with quotations respectively from Pythagoras (Cicero, *De officiis* I xvii 16) and from Aristotle, *Nicomachean Ethics* XVIII, 7, 1158°, 1–10. See also *Convivio* I viii 12: Dante speaks of friendship throughout the *Convivio*. See also entries on 'amicizia', 'amico', 'amistà', 'amistanza' by E. Pasquini in *Enciclopedia dantesca*, I, 203–08 and 210–12.

[77] See *Inferno* XX, 23, 'torta'; *Inferno* XXV, 77, 'perversa'.

[78] Cf. in *Inferno* VI the punishment of the gluttons, which prompts Virgil to speak of the Last Judgement and the resurrection of the damned after they have returned to their 'trista tomba'.

[79] The tree of XXII, 139–41, seems to reappear in XXIV, 112–17, where it is explicitly identified as generated from the tree of knowledge of good and evil 'that was eaten of by Eve'. Casini–Barbi see the first tree (canto XXII) as the tree of life, and the second (canto XXIV) as the tree of knowledge, while most commentators see them as one and the same. In canto XXIII, 73, however, Forese uses the plural form 'alberi'.

[80] For all of these, Peter Lombard, *Liber Sententiarum* II, Dist. XXI, 5, 6.

[81] *Poetics* 11, 1452a 31–32: 'recognition ... is a passage from ignorance to knowledge, which produces friendship or enmity in those who are destined to fortune or misfortune (*pros eutykhian e dystykhian*)'.

[82] See *Convivio* III xv 12; III vi 13.

[83] In parallel to this partly obscure prophecy in *Purgatorio* XXIII, 97–111, on Florentine women there is the one in *Purgatorio* XXIV, 82–90, concerning Corso's death and damnation in Hell. These prophecies, both uttered by Forese, are the two occasions in which lost time moves from the mainly personal dimension explored in the two cantos to the general historical dimension of time predicted rather than regained.

[84] *Inferno* XV, 79–85, 49–54; *Purgatorio* XXIII, 115–17, 118–33. The prophetic invective against the women of Florence (*Purgatorio* XXIII, 94–111) is also paralleled in Brunetto's attack against 'l'ingrato popolo maligno' (*Inferno* XV, 61–69). Note the inversion in the scenic distribution of themes.

[85] Thomas Aquinas, *In Aristotelis ... De memoria et reminiscentia commentarium*, 301; see the Latin text of Aristotle, ibid., 1, 159–63, 32, and the Greek one at 1449b 4–9 and 1451a 20-b 6. See also *Convivio* I viii 12, II ii 4, IV ix 11, IV xiv 10, for the references in Vasoli's notes on Aristotle's works and the commentaries of Albert the Great and Thomas. For a more in-depth treatment, see M. J. Carruthers, *The Book of Memory. A Study of Memory in Medieval Culture* (Cambridge: Cambridge University Press, 1990), pp. 46–79 and 185–87. On the 'memorar', see G. Savarese, 'Una proposta per Forese: Dante e il "memorar presente"', *Rassegna della Letteratura Italiana*, 94 (1990), 5–20 (pp. 19–20).

[86] *De memoria et reminiscentia* 1453a 10–14 (II, 208–09); Thomas, 398 ff.

[87] *Prior Analytics* 67a 22–27.

[88] The controversy over the *tenzone* has on the one hand those who argue its non-authenticity, especially D. Guerri, *La corrente popolare nel Rinascimento. Berte, burle e baie nella Firenze del Brunellesco e del Burchiello* (Florence: Sansoni, 1931); A. Lanza, *Polemiche e berte letterarie nella Firenze del primo Quattrocento* (Rome: Bulzoni, 1972); M. Cursietti, *La falsa tenzone di Dante con Forese Donati* (Anzio: De Rubeis, 1995); R. Stefanini, 'Tenzone sì tenzone no', *Lectura Dantis Virginiana*, 18–19 (1996), 111–28; E. Esposito, 'Tenzone no', *La parola del testo*, 1 (1997), 268–71; A. Lanza, 'A norma di filologia: ancora a proposito della cosiddetta Tenzone tra Dante e Forese', *L'Alighieri*, 38 (1997), 43–54; M. Cursietti, 'Dante e Forese alla taverna del Panico: le prove documentate della falsità della tenzone', *L'Alighieri*, 41 (2000), 1–22. On the other hand, and I believe conclusively, there is M. Barbi, *Problemi di critica dantesca. Seconda serie*, pp. 87–214; and M. Marti, 'Rime realistiche (la tenzone e le petrose dantesche)', *Nuove letture dantesche*, 8 vols (Florence: Le Monnier, 1968–76), VIII (1976), 209–30. See also F. Alfie, 'For want of a nail: the Guerri–Lanza–Cursietti argument regarding the *Tenzone*', *Dante Studies*, 116 (1998), 141–59; and F. Chiappelli, 'Proposta d'interpretazione per la tenzone di Dante con Forese Donati', and 'Postilla al nodo Salomone', now in his *Il legame musaico*, ed. by P. M. Forni (Rome: Edizioni di Storia e Letteratura, 1984), pp. 41–73. Most scholars now tend to recognize the authenticity of the *tenzone*: see G. Contini, in *Un'idea di Dante* (Turin: Einaudi, 1976), pp. 51–53, and Dante Alighieri, *Rime*, II 1047–51. None of the arguments against seems to me particularly persuasive, and I try here to offer some linguistic evidence in support of the authenticity argument.

[89] Some will inevitably see Forese's 'non *contendere*' in canto XXIII, 48, as an allusion to the *tenzone*, and the 'anella sanza gemme' as a rather oblique reference to Dante's marriage to Gemma Donati: 'che 'nnanellata pria disposando [l]'avea con la sua gemma'!

[90] I have always thought that Forese's allusions in the *tenzone* to Alighiero's 'knot' had to do with debts — 'of money gained by usury' — (contracted perhaps with the Donati family, just as Dante's were with his father-in-law Manetto). Support for this line of thought is found in Dante Alighieri, *Rime*, ed. by G. Contini (Turin: Einaudi, 1946), p. 85. In his reproach in *Va' rivesti San Gal*, 'se tu ci hai per mendichi, perché pur mandi a noi per caritate?' Forese is clearly accusing Dante of continually running to the Donati for help (and so the sonnet's closure is all the more ferocious, with Forese seeing Dante go begging 'a lo spedale a Pinti', a hospital founded and supported by the Donati). Similarly, I suspect that Dante's irony, in *Bicci novel*, on the 'someone' who is 'lying in his sorry bed' ('tal giace per lui nel letto tristo') is an indirect reference not only to Forese's 'putative' father, Simone, but also to Simone convincing Gianni Schicchi to 'counterfeit in himself Buoso Donati' on his deathbed (*Inferno* XXX, 42–45). In any case, I believe the *tenzone* needs to be read within the framework of the complex relationships between Dante and the Donati family: see S. Noakes, 'Virility, nobility, and banking: the crossing of discourses in the *Tenzone* with Forese', in *Dante for the New Millennium*, ed. by T. Barolini and H. Wayne Storey (New York: Fordham University Press, 2003), pp. 241–58.

[91] On this point Ginsberg's formulation is particularly lucid, in *Dante's Aesthetics of Being*, pp. 82–104 (pp. 96–99).

[92] Ginsberg, ibid.; see also G. Mazzotta, *Dante, Poet of the Desert* (Princeton: Princeton University Press, 1979), pp. 201–02. On Bonagiunta's 'knot', see G. Gorni's persuasive arguments in *Il nodo della lingua e il verbo d'amore: studi su Dante e altri duecentisti* (Florence: Olschki, 1981); and in particular L. Pertile, 'Il nodo di Bonagiunta, le penne di Dante e il Dolce Stil Novo', *Lettere Italiane*, 46 (1994), 44–75, now in his *La punta del disio* (Florence: Cadmo, 2005), pp. 85–113.

[93] Meaning of course that she had — as Foster and Boyde translate with the right ambiguity — 'other troubles': the word 'voglia' indicates another kind of desire.

[94] See K. Foster and P. Boyde, *Dante's Lyric Poetry*, II, 251, n. 7.

[95] Gregory, *Moralia in Iob* XXXI, 45, 88; Thomas, *De malo*, q. 14, a. 4 resp.; *Summa Theologiae* II, II, q. 149, a. 6.

[96] E. Sanguineti, now in *Il realismo di Dante* (Florence: Sansoni, 1976²), pp. 65–102, on p. 92; see also R. Abrams, 'Inspiration and gluttony: the moral context of Dante's poetics of the "Sweet New Style"', *Modern Language Notes*, 91 (1976), 30–59.

[97] See V. Russo, '*Pg XXIII*: Forese o la maschera del discorso', in his *Il romanzo teologico*, pp. 125–44 (p. 134).

[98] Ibid., pp. 135–36; see T. Barolini, *Dante's Poets. Textuality and Truth in the Comedy* (Princeton: Princeton University Press, 1984), pp. 45–98.

[99] Translation by Foster and Boyde, *Dante's Lyric Poetry*, I, 151.

[100] Dante Alighieri, *Rime*, ed. by G. Contini, p. 82.

[101] As R. Hollander notes, 'Dante's *dolce stil novo* and the Comedy', in *Dante: mito e poesia*, ed. by M. Picone and T. Crivelli (Florence: Cesati, 1999), pp. 263–81 (p. 273), whose deductions partly differ from my own. See also the discussion ibid., pp. 296–313.

[102] *Vita nuova* XIX 2. The tongue which speaks 'come per sé mossa' is, as Durling–Martinez rightly notes (p. 413), a version of Psalm 50 (the *Miserere*), verse 17: 'Domine labia mea aperies, et os meum adnuntiabit *laudem* tuam': the same line as sung by the gluttons in *Purgatorio* XXIII.

[103] The 'dictator Deus' of *Monarchia*, III iv 11. For this see Durling–Martinez, *Purgatorio*, pp. 413–14 and references therein, in particular R. Hollander, 'Dante's *dolce stil novo*', and R. M. Durling, '*Mio figlio ov'è? (Inf. x, 60)*', in *Dante: da Firenze all'aldilà*, ed. by M. Picone (Florence: Cesati, 2001), pp. 303–29.

[104] As M. Casella pointed out seventy years ago in *Studi danteschi*, 18 (1934), 101–26 (p. 108). Note in particular the last line of Ivo's passage: 'tunc vera et veneranda doctrina est, cum quod lingua loquitur conscientia dictat, caritas suggerit et spiritus ingerit': Ives, *Epître a Séverin sur la charité*, Richard de Saint-Victor, *Les Quatre degrés de la violente charité*, crit. ed. by G. Dumeige (Paris: Vrin, 1955), p. 45 (I, 15–17): see below, n. 142.

[105] Exodus 3. 14; see R. L. Martinez, 'The pilgrim's answer to Bonagiunta and the poetics of the spirit', *Stanford Italian Review*, 4 (1983), 37–63; 1 Corinthians 15. 10; *Inferno* II, 32; *Paradiso* I, 5–6: 2 Corinthians 12. 2.

[106] *Purgatorio* XXI, 11 – XXVI, 70.

[107] Here I refer to, and partly modify, the view set out in my '*Trattando l'ombre come cosa salda*: fisiologia, metafisica e poetica dell'ombra', in *Elogio dell'ombra*, ed. by S. Colmagro (Venice: Marsilio, 1995), pp. 33–47.

[108] *Inferno* VI, 36.

[109] Put clearly by Dante the character in XXV, 20–21: 'Come si può far magro là dove l'uopo di nodrir non tocca?'.

[110] See Boyde, *Dante Philomythes*, pp. 270–81; *Perception and Passion*, pp. 140–45.

[111] As pointed out by several commentators, including Z. Barański in his important '*Purgatorio* XXV', *Lectura Dantis Turicensis, Purgatorio*, ed. by G. Güntert and M. Picone (Florence: Cesati, 2001), pp. 389–406, it is interesting to note that according to Thomas angels can take on 'corpora ex aere, condensando ipsum virtute divina, quantum necesse est ad corporis assumendi formationem': *Summa Theologiae* I, q. 51, a. 2, ad 3. On Dante's shades, see F. Tollemache and D. Consoli, 'ombra', in *Enciclopedia Dantesca*, IV (1973), 141–45; B. Nardi, 'L'origine dell'anima umana secondo Dante', in his *Studi di filosofia medievale* (Rome: Edizioni di Storia e Letteratura, 1960), pp. 9–68; S. Battaglia, 'La teoria della generazione e il mito dell'anima', in his *La poesia dottrinale del Purgatorio* (Naples: Liguori, 1964), pp. 87–115; E. Gilson, 'Qu'est-ce qu'une ombre' and '*Ombre* et *luci* dans la Divine Commedie', in his *Dante et Béatrice. Études dantesques* (Paris: Vrin, 1974), pp. 23–65. V. Russo, 'A proposito del canto XXV del *Purgatorio*', in *Esperienze e/di letture dantesche (tra il 1966 e il 1970)* (Naples: Liguori, 1971), pp. 101–58; N. Lindheim, 'Body, soul, and immortality: some readings in Dante's *Commedia*', *Modern Language Notes*, 105 (1990), 1–32; M. Cogan, *The Design in the Wax* (Notre Dame–London: University of Notre Dame Press, 1999), pp. 119–47; R. M. Durling, 'The body and the flesh in the *Purgatorio*', and M. Gragnolati, 'From plurality to (near) unicity of forms: embryology in *Purgatorio* 25', in *Dante for the New Millennium*, pp. 183–210.

[112] *Purgatorio* III, 28–33.

[113] Which certainly does not preclude divine 'Virtù' being the ultimate cause of the whole process, although Statius does not mention it.

[114] This metamorphosis is naturally in direct contrast to the snake metamorphoses in the parallel canto, *Inferno* XXV.

[115] Chiavacci Leonardi *ad Purgatorio* XXV, 101.

[116] *Aeneid* VI, 733: in the recognition scene between Aeneas and Anchises after death, Anchises explains that the body is the cause of the soul's 'fear and desire, sorrow and joy'.

[117] *Inferno* VI, 94–111; *Paradiso* XIV, 43–60: see A. M. Chiavacci Leonardi, '*Le bianche stole*: il tema della resurrezione nel *Paradiso*', in *Dante e la Bibbia*, ed. by G. Barblan (Florence: Olschki, 1988), pp. 249–71; on the other hand, L. Battaglia Ricci, 'Piccarda, o della carità: lettura del terzo canto del *Paradiso*', *Filologia e critica*, 14 (1989), 27–70, n. 13 (pp. 41–42). The problem of the lights of Paradise, for which see *Paradiso* XXII, 58–63 and XXX, 43–45, strikes me as different: while in the Empyrean it is possible for Dante to see them as they will be seen on Judgement Day, after the resurrection of the flesh, nothing of this sort is predicated of the infernal or repentant shades. Cf. J. A. Scott, 'Canto XXXI', in *Paradiso, Lectura Dantis Turicensis*, pp. 473–89 (p. 475).

[118] For the figural concept of *umbra*, see E. Auerbach, 'Figura', in his *Scenes from the Drama of European Literature* (Manchester: Manchester University Press, 1984), pp. 11–76, and in particular pp. 28–60; but in conjunction with A. C. Charity's critique in *Events and their Afterlife. The Dialectics of Christian Typology in the Bible and Dante* (Cambridge: Cambridge University Press, 1966), pp. 179–207; and J. Pépin, *Dante et la tradition de l'allégorie* (Montreal: Institut d'Etudes médiévales, 1970), pp. 31–51. The 'ombra' used for Paradise in *Paradiso* (e.g. I, 22–24) seems to differ somewhat: for which — and for its Bonaventurean antecedents — see Z. Barański, 'I segni di Dante', *Dante e i segni: saggi per una storia intellettuale di Dante Alighieri* (Naples: Liguori, 2000), x + 231 pp., in particular pp. 70–76.

[119] *Purgatorio* XXXI, 139–41: Wisdom 7. 26; see *Convivio* III xv 1–5 (on *Amor che ne la mente mi ragiona*, 55), *Vita nuova* XIX, 20 (on *Donne ch'avete intelletto d'amore*, the 'song' of *Purgatorio* XXIV, 51). This is certainly a moment of pre-paradisiacal revelation, but the lines concern *all* the poet's work: choosing, together with the decanting of the Castalian water, the *shade* of Parnassus seems significant: all the more so since becoming 'pale' in the shade is a carefully-chosen image. The shade of the mount of the Muses would in fact suffice to make anyone go pale, that is, would drain a poet attempting the task of treating shades as 'solid things'.

[120] The Greek term *skiá* (*umbra*) is used in highly significant contexts in Colossians 2. 17, Hebrews 8. 5 and 10. 1; see Hebrews 9. 11; 1 Corinthians 10. 5–6; Galatians 4. 21–31; Romans 5. 14.

[121] *Paradiso* III, 85; *Purgatorio* XXIV, 141.

[122] For the historical details, see E. Levi, *Piccarda e Gentucca: studi e ricerche dantesche* (Bologna: Zanichelli, 1921).

[123] On the link between Piccarda (who took the name of Constance along with her vows) and Constance, and the theme of inconstancy, see G. Mazzotta, 'Teologia ed esegesi biblica (*Par.* III–v)' in *Dante e la Bibbia*, ed. by G. Barblan (Florence: Olschki, 1988), pp. 95–112 (pp. 103–04).

[124] See J. Freccero, *Dante. The Poetics of Conversion*, ed. by R. Jacoff (Cambridge, MA: Harvard University Press, 1986), pp. 221–24; and T. Barolini, *The Undivine Comedy. Detheologizing Dante* (Princeton: Princeton University Press, 1992), pp. 166–93; on the Empyrean, B. Nardi, *Saggi di filosofia dantesca* (Florence: La Nuova Italia, 1967²), pp. 167–214.

[125] The theme and image of God-the-Bridegroom (Christ) derive of course from the Song of Songs and from its traditional interpretations in conjunction with the Gospels: Matthew 9. 15, 27. 1–13; John 3. 29. The earthly bridegroom–celestial bridegroom contrast, which Dante implicitly indicates in *Paradiso* III, might have been inspired by Clare's own writings, in particular by her letters to Agnes of Bohemia, who rejected marriage to Frederick II in order to wed Christ: see *La Letteratura Francescana*, I: *Francesco e Chiara d'Assisi*, ed. by C. Leonardi (Milan: Mondadori–Fondazione Valla, 2004), pp. 300–01, 15.

[126] *Purgatorio* XXIII, 128: Dante seems to take for granted that his old friend knows who Beatrice is, and what she means and has meant to him. Beatrice's name is mentioned only to Forese among all the souls encountered by the pilgrim in the afterlife: and see commentary by Chiavacci Leonardi on *Purgatorio* XXIII, 128–30.

[127] See A. Chiari, 'Il canto di Piccarda e il preludio del *Paradiso* dantesco', now in his *Nove canti danteschi*, Varese: Magenta, 1966; M. Marti, *Realismo dantesco*, pp. 80–91. On the whole episode, see M. Fubini, s.v. 'Donati, Piccarda', in *Enciclopedia dantesca*, II, 565–68.

[128] Among modern critics, the first interpretation is found in, for example, Scartazzini–Vandelli, Casini–Barbi, Sapegno, Mattalia, Singleton, Pasquini–Quaglio, Chiavacci Leonardi; the second in Tommaseo, Momigliano, and Pietrobono. Benvenuto is among the first. Buti, Landino, and Vellutello take 'primo foco' to mean 'cielo della Luna'.

[129] See R. Stefanini, '*III*', in '*Dante's Divine Comedy*. Introductory readings, III: *Paradiso*', *Lectura Dantis Virginiana*, 16–17 (1995), 30–45.

[130] 'Colpo di glottide': Contini, *Un'idea di Dante*, p. 125.

[131] Dante is careful to point out the nature of the shade twice in the canto, in lines 34 and 67. Lines 16 and 48–49 show that the face is visible. In the second and third Heavens there seem to be corporeal semblances in the spirits of the blessed, albeit concealed by the light radiating from them: *Paradiso* V, 106–08, 124–29 (Justinian), and VIII, 52–54 (Charles Martel); and see also p. 38.

[132] *Paradiso* XIX, 64–66. See C. Moevs, *The Metaphysics of Dante's Comedy* (New York–Oxford: Oxford University Press, 2005), p. 129; *contra*, for a possible slip on Dante's part, see Gilson, *Dante et Béatrice*, p. 62.

[133] That 'margarita' means not only 'precious stone' but also 'pearl' is barely worth demonstrating: it has illustrious precedents in the Vulgate New Testament (Matthew 7. 6, 18. 46; 1 Timothy 2. 9; Revelation 17. 4, 18. 12, 21. 21), in Hugutio (*Derivationes*, M 86, 9, p. 755 in Uguccione da Pisa, *Derivationes*, II, ed. by E. Cecchini et al., Tavarnuzze: SISMEL-Galluzzo, 2004: 'margarita' significantly 'a mare'), and in Dante, *Convivio* IV XXX 4. On the 'segni bui' of the Moon, see B. Nardi, *Saggi di filosofia dantesca*, pp. 3–39.

[134] *Paradiso* II, 31–36: see G. Stabile, 'Navigazione celeste e simbolismo lunare in *Par.* II', *Studi medievali*, 30 (1980), 97–140.

[135] *Commedia di Dante Alighieri con ragionamenti e note di Niccolò Tommaseo* (Milan: Rejna, 1854), p. 558.

[136] Thus Ovid's *Metamorphoses* is the subtext linking *Inferno* XXV, *Purgatorio* XXIII, and *Paradiso* III.

[137] 1 Corinthians 13. 12, at the end of the famous 'hymn' to charity which Dante certainly bore in mind for Piccarda's celebration of it.

[138] See Barolini, *The Undivine Comedy*, pp. 166–74; K. Stierle, 'Canto III', in *Lectura Dantis Turicensis*, III, *Paradiso*, ed. by G. Güntert and M. Picone (Florence: Cesati, 2002), pp. 53–67. Tommaseo's concision regarding the three cantos (p. 563) is admirable: 'Nel primo del Paradiso è posta la dottrina dell'ordine, e strumento dell'ordine è posto l'amore; nel secondo, l'idea dell'ordine viene applicata ai moti de' cieli e all'intelligenze che li muovono amando, e alla gioia che da essi traluce come viva pupilla; nel terzo mostrasi l'amore come vincolo alla società de' beati e forma di loro beatitudine'.

[139] On this point, see *The Tragic and the Sublime*, pp. 250–78.

[140] Matthew 5. 9; John 14. 27; Luke 2. 14 and 19. 38; Romans 14. 17; 1 Corinthians 13. 1–8; 1 John 4. 7–8.

[141] Augustine, *Confessions*, I i 6–8, XIII ix 10; *De civitate Dei* XXII xxix e xxx; XIX xiii. See E. Gardner, *Dante and the Mystics* (London: Dent, 1913), pp. 178–85; C. F. Goffis, 'Il canto I del *Paradiso*', in *Lectura Dantis Scaligera*, III (Florence: Le Monnier, 1971), pp. 1–32.

[142] For these references, see the major works by R. Migliorini Fissi, 'La nozione di *deificatio* nel *Paradiso*', *Letture classensi*, 9/10 (1982), 39–72; S. Botterill, *Dante and the Mystical Tradition. Bernard of Clairvaux in the Commedia* (Cambridge: Cambridge University Press, 1994), in particular pp. 238–41; M. Colombo, *Dai mistici a Dante: il linguaggio dell'ineffabilità* (Florence: La Nuova Italia, 1987), pp. 73–89; L. Battaglia Ricci, 'Piccarda, o della carità'. Battaglia Ricci rightly focuses on Ivo's *Epistle*, in particular pointing out (p. 52) how Dante may have been inspired by it here as well as in *Purgatorio* XXIV, 52–54 ('"I' mi son un …"'), and perhaps also in *De vulgari eloquentia* I iv–v: see above, n. 104.

[143] Clare of Assisi, *Epistola III ad sanctam Agnetem de Praga*, 13, in *Letteratura francescana*, I, 292–93.

[144] Bonaventure, *Breviloquium* VII 7 1–3.

[145] Thomas Aquinas, *Summa Theologiae* I–II, q. 2 resp.; I–II, q. 3, a. 4 ad 1 e 8c; I–II, q. 70 a. 3; II–II, q. 29, a. 2, 4, resp. e ad 3, ad 4; Suppl. q. 93, a. 2 *contra*, a. 3, *contra*, resp., ad 1; *In librum Beati Dionysii de divinis nominibus Expositio* XI, l. 1, 891.

[146] See G. Güntert, 'Dante e Piccarda o la parola come immagine perfetta', in G. Güntert et al., *Orbis mediaevalis: mélanges … offerts à Raudolf Bezzola …* (Berne: Francke, 1978), pp. 149–62.

[147] T. S. Eliot, *Dante* (London: Faber, 1965, first publ. 1929), p. 46. Eliot uses Piccarda's words in 'Cooking Egg' in *Poems 1920*, and again at the end of *Ash-Wednesday*.

[148] D. Walcott, *The Bounty*, I (London–Boston: Faber, 1997), 3–4.

[149] J. Took, *L'Etterno Piacer. Aesthetic Ideas in Dante* (Oxford: Clarendon Press, 1984). My debt towards this book will be evident in the paragraphs that follow. Dante's variations on the theme of 'etterno piacer' start in *Purgatorio* XXIX, 32, and XXXI, 52, and are developed in *Paradiso*: XVIII, 16; XX, 77; XXXIII, 33.

[150] *Paradiso* IV, 34–36.

[151] *Paradiso* XXVIII, 108.

[152] *Paradiso* III, 32.

[153] Thomas Aquinas, *Quaestiones disputatae* I, *De veritate*, q. 22, a 1, ad 11–12. See the other passages cited by Took, *L'Etterno Piacer*, p. 98, n. 46; his general treatment, pp. 31–35, 38–41. For the aesthetic theories of Thomas Aquinas, see also U. Eco, *Il problema estetico in Tommaso d'Aquino* (Milan: Bompiani, 1970²).

[154] Images of the desire for food, 'gola' (and cf. Forese) and satiety in *Paradiso* III, 91–93; IV, 1–6; V, 37–39.

[155] Thomas Aquinas, *Summa Theologiae* I, q. 73, a. 1, resp.: and see Took, *L'Etterno Piacer*, pp. 1–2, 24–29.

[156] *Paradiso* XXXIII, 91.

[157] *Paradiso* XXVII, 88 (see *Convivio* IV xiii 2 and Vasoli's note; *Convivio* II xiv 19–20 and III xv 6–7); *Paradiso* V, 89 ('cupido ingegno'). For all this see B. Nardi, *Dante e la cultura medievale* (Bari: Laterza, 1942), pp. 100–47, and the fundamental essay by K. Foster, 'The mind in love: Dante's philosophy', in *Dante. A Collection of Critical Essays*, ed. by J. Freccero (Englewood Cliffs, NJ: Prentice Hall, 1965), pp. 43–60.

[158] The themes of divine will and human run throughout cantos III–V; 'volontà' and 'voto' are 'etymologically' linked according to Thomas, *Summa Theologiae* II–II q. 88 I ad 2: see G. Mazzotta, *Teologia ed esegesi biblica*, pp. 101–02.

[159] *Paradiso* IV, 124–32. See B. Nardi, *Dal Convivio alla Commedia* (Rome, 1960), pp. 75–83; M. E. Frank, 'La "concreata e perpetua sete" del *Paradiso*', *Esperienze letterarie*, 18 (1993), 41–55; L. Pertile, '*Paradiso*: a drama of desire', in *Word and Drama in Dante*, ed. by J. C. Barnes and J. Petrie (Dublin: Foundation for Italian Studies, 1993), pp. 143–80; id., 'La punta del disio: storia di una metafora dantesca', *Lectura Dantis Virginiana*, 7 (1990), 3–28.

[160] *Purgatorio* XXI, 1–3: compared with the passage in *Paradiso* IV, this *terzina* underlines that the 'sete natural' can only be satisfied by divine grace.

[161] Both are linked to the image of food and the search for it.

[162] See the exhaustive treatment in S. Vanni Rovighi, 'Il canto IV del *Paradiso* visto da uno studioso di filosofia medievale', *Studi danteschi*, 48 (1971), 67–82; P. Giannantonio, 'La poesia dottrinale (*Paradiso* IV)', *Critica letteraria*, 8 (1980), 3–23; Boyde, *Perception and Passion*, pp. 193–209; L. Pertile, *IV*, in *Dante's Divine Comedy. Introductory Readings*, III, *Paradiso*, pp. 46–67.

[163] At *Paradiso* IV, 39, instead of Petrocchi's 'celestial' I read 'spiritual', following E. G. Parodi, *Poesia e storia nella Divina Commedia* (Vicenza: Neri Pozza, 1965), pp. 377–78. Parodi cites a passage from Thomas Aquinas (*Summa Theologiae* III, *Supplementum*, q. 93 a. 2, 2) in support of his reading.

[164] *Paradiso* IV, 40–51; see Boyde, *Dante Philomythes*, pp. 205–07; on this pssage and cantos III–IV of *Paradiso* see the important considerations surrounding the themes of sacrifice and grammar in G. Mazzotta, now in *Dante's Vision and the Circle of Knowledge* (Princeton: Princeton University Press, 1993), pp. 34–55.

[165] See the material and discussion in *Vedere l'invisibile: Nicea e lo statuto dell'Immagine*, ed. by L. Russo (Palermo: Aesthetica, 1999²).

[166] For the references to Gregory the Great and Richard of St Victor, see Pertile, *IV*, p. 65, n. 19; Barański, *Dante e i segni*, pp. 1–2, 35–39.

[167] *De divinis nominibus* 597 A–B; I, l. III, 8, 27: see Took, *L'Etterno Piacer*, p. 97, n. 34.

[168] Thomas Aquinas, *In librum beati Dionysii*, I, l. III, 102–05; *Summa Theologiae* I, q. 1, a. 9 resp., ad 1–3; q. 1, a. 10, ad 3.

[169] Mazzotta, *Dante's Vision and the Circle of Knowledge*, p. 47, cites Isidore, *Etymologiae* I, xxxii, 22: 'aliud enim sonat et aliud intelligitur'.

[170] As far as God himself is concerned, the exceptions are the 'braccia' of *Purgatorio* III, 122 (perhaps the stretched ones of the crucified Christ); the 'faccia' of *Purgatorio* III, 126 (meaning the 'aspect', the mercy); the creating 'mano' of *Purgatorio* XVI, 85; the 'occhio' of *Paradiso* X, 12; and the 'faccia' of *Paradiso* XXIX, 77. Work on Dante's anthropomorphism (particularly as regards the angels) remains to be done. As V. Montemaggi notes in '"La rosa in che il verbo divino carne si fece": human bodies and truth in the poetic narrative of the *Commedia*', forthcoming in *Dante and the Human Body*, ed. by J. C. Barnes and M. Sonzogni (Dublin: Irish Academic Press), it does not seem to be by chance that the highest concentration of theological anthropomorphic images occurs in *Purgatorio* III, the canto where Dante's explicit meditation on the souls' corporeality begins and where, at lines 94–111, the bodies of both Manfredi and Dante himself are presented in a Christological key.

[171] For the distinction between the two see *The Tragic and the Sublime*, pp. 230–32.

[172] See *De vulgari eloquentia*, in particular II vii.

[173] See Mazzotta, *Dante's Vision*, pp. 47–48.

[174] See R. Jacoff, '*Shadowy Prefaces*: an Introduction to *Paradiso*', in *The Cambridge Companion to Dante* ed. by R. Jacoff (Cambridge-New York: Cambridge University Press, 1993), pp. 208–25.

[175] *Paradiso* V, 122–23.

[176] *Paradiso* IV, 28. The theme of *deificatio* in this sense stems from Dionysius. In both *De coelesti hierarchia* and *De divinis nominibus* the Areopagite brings it to the fore several times. In the latter, in particular, at 589C § 3. 12, 597A § 8. 27, 649C § 11. 75, 893A § 4. 338, 956A § 6. 426. For the last case see Thomas Aquinas, *In librum beati Dionysii*, XI, l. IV, 938: '[Dionysius] dicit quod non oportet de praemissis dubitare, cum aliqui ex doctoribus divinae et christianae religionis … hoc ipsum dicant, scilicet quod bonitas et Deitas omnibus supereminens, est causa *ipsius per se deitatis et bonitatis*, nominantes *per se bonitatem* quoddam *donum ex Deo proveniens* per quod entia sunt bona; *et* per se *deitatem* quoddam Dei donum, per quod aliqui fiunt participative dii; et

similiter nominant *per se pulchritudinem*, ipsam *effusionem* pulchritudinis per quam causatur et universalis et particularis pulchritudo in rebus et per quam fiunt aliqua et universaliter et particulariter *pulchra*'.

[177] On Ovid in Dante see the whole of the second part of the volume edited by R. Jacoff and J. Schnapp, *The Poetry of Allusion. Virgil and Ovid in Dante's Commedia* (Stanford: Stanford University Press, 1991); M. Picone, *Dante argonauta. La ricezione dei miti ovidiani nella Commedia*, in *Ovidius redivivus. Von Ovid zu Dante*, ed. by M. Picone and B. Zimmermann (Stuttgart: M. & P., 1994), pp. 173–202; P. S. Hawkins, *Dante's Testaments: Essays in Scriptural Imagination* (Stanford: Stanford University Press, 1999), pp. 145–58; J. Schnapp, 'Trasfigurazione e metamorfosi nel *Paradiso* dantesco', in *Dante e la Bibbia*, pp. 273–92.

[178] See Took, *L'Etterno Piacer*, pp. 1–2.

[179] On corporeality in the *Commedia*, see the important essay by R. Jacoff, '"Our bodies, our selves": the body in the *Commedia*', in *Sparks and Seeds: Medieval Literature and Its Afterlife. Essays in honor of John Freccero*, ed. by D. E. Stewart and A. Cornish (Turnhout: Brepols, 2000), pp. 119–37.

[180] *Purgatorio* XXIII, 37, 59–60.

[181] *Purgatorio* XXVII, 104–05; *Paradiso* XXXII, 7–9.

INDEX

[For ease of consultation, names mentioned in the notes are referred to by note-number rather than page]

53